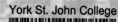

Published by Hawthorn Press, Hawthorn House,
1 Lansdown Lane, Stroud, Gloucestershire, GL5 1BJ, UK
Tel: (01453) 757040 Fax: (01453) 751138
email: info@hawthornpress.com
Website: **www.hawthornpress.com**

Drawings and cover illustration © Judith Evans
Cover design and typesetting by Hawthorn Press, Stroud, Glos.
Printed by The Bath Press, Bath

Printed on environmentally friendly chlorine-free paper manufactured from renewable forest stock

Acknowledgements
Brandon Books, Dingle, for their kind permission to use extracts from *To School Through the Fields* by Alice Taylor, 1988.
Mercia Press, Cork, Ireland, for their kind permission to use the extract from *Once in a Green Summer* by Thomas F. Walsh

British Library Cataloguing in Publication Data applied for

ISBN 1 903458 23 4

Contents

Preface

We live in a world normally punctuated by two festivals each year: Christmas and Easter. Both are extravagant events, often creating as much turmoil as celebration, and costing the earth to get through. What a treat to come upon a book as simple as it is rich. *Celebrating Irish Festivals* is a book about festivals that have their source in Irish soil and have grown up through popular celebration to become community events that mark and cherish the changing year. Each festival is coloured by related crafts and activities, and nourished by easy-to-cook seasonal recipes. Just as stories have been around before man could write, so too the joy of these annual rituals rely on a heritage that goes back to a time when honouring the yearly cycles connected people on earth to the earth itself. Myth and legend gave voice to this connection. We have never lost the need to be connected. The stories selected in the book are the salt and pepper in the stew that fills a hungry heart as only stories can.

In my years as a teacher and storyteller I have become aware that when moments in the year are made special by telling the right story for the occasion, children and adults alike come to appreciate the world around them in a more meaningful way. This book is a collection of festivals that give rise to a deeper appreciation of the world. They make space for what is out of the ordinary and give flavour to what may otherwise become bland.

Our lives can start to seem like a race against the clock, but this book is a meander through Irish-time, where there's always time for playing games, sharing a tale, noticing beauty in its place and dipping the cup of celebration to those lucky enough to be passing.

Alexander Mackenzie, Storyteller

Acknowledgements

Padraigin Ni Uallachan for the music for *Carul na Nollag, Casadh Cam na Feadarnai* and *Amhran na Bealtaine* from '*A Stor 's a Stóirín*' {Gael Linn CEFCD 166}

Nickomo for the tune for *May the Road Rise with You*

Jonathon Angus for the music for *Curoo, Curoo*

Tony Buckley of the Ulster Folk and Transport Museum for advice

Pete Brown for advice on the midsummer sunwheel

Kathleen Byrne whose simulated Newgrange sunrise I have adapted and included

Carole Guyett for herbal recipes

Noreen Kennedy for her Auntie Cissy's memories

Melanie Lorien for teaching me how to make a variety of harvest knots

Colm McLochlainn for his advice on spelling

Lesley Merriman for the idea for the Michaelmas dragon

Denise Moroney for her suggestion for a Martinmas giveaway

Sean O Duinn for advice

Caitriona Patience for her story of the Easter hare

Imelda Smyth, Brenda Mahon and Peader O'Huallaigh for support

Angie Pinson, Samantha Fairchild, Shakti and Cian for listening to the stories

Iain for inspiration

Foreword

One evening, early in November, as the days finally darken into true winter and long after school has ended for the day, the cars return to the car park of Raheen Wood School in East Clare. The children gather, hushed by the darkness and the strange, expectant mood as lanterns are lit and they begin their walk through the school grounds and into the forest that stretches below the school to the lake. Quiet voices join in the singing of the lantern song, and once again the creatures of the woods and the ancient oak trees must pause to wonder that this year they are being visited once more by these beautiful lanterns lighting up the dark night, and children's voices singing:

I go with my little lantern,
my lantern is going with me

In Heaven the stars are shining;
on earth shines my lantern with me

My light shines bright through all the night,
la bim-ba, la bim-ba, la bim

My light grows dim, we must go in,
la bim-ba, la bim-ba, la bim

This is the festival of St Martin, better known to the children as the lantern festival and it marks a special moment in the rhythm of the year, as we move towards a time of outer dark and brightness within doors.

Such a festival, taking its place in the round of the year, creates a deeply satisfying sense of belonging in children. Just as the life of the community is strengthened by annual festivals, so all of life is carried in a rhythmic embrace. Whether it be the beating of the heart or breathing in and out, all rhythmic life has a quality that sustains and enlivens us. In the leaves of the plant, in tumbling waters of a stream, even in the clouds in the sky we can discern rhythm – and where there is rhythm there is life and health.

Most of the festivals in this book are public or social events, intended to be celebrated by the community, and they will repay the community any investment of time and effort, as will the more private, family festivals. Birthdays, of course, are the most obvious but each family will find events that can be celebrated to mark moments of particular importance. These private festivals can be simple events but will again repay any investment of time and effort and over the years become an essential part of family identity and memory.

This book focuses on festivals in Ireland where we pride ourselves on some intangible social quality that makes life here attractive and special. In recent years there's been a growing sense that we are losing this quality; and it is perhaps foolhardy to think that special qualities we may have had in the past will survive the onslaught of commercial and technical pressures without some action on our part. Celebrating festivals together is an obvious and appropriate action we can all take as families and communities, and this book provides a perfect basis from which we can build a more human social life.

I never celebrated the lantern festival as a child; it is really a new (or perhaps renewed) festival in Ireland. But I do remember as a ten-year-old child, far from home in Connemara as a Gael-Linn 'scholar', running from home to home in Teach Mor on St Brigit's day, in early spring, with bundles of

rushes, singing and reciting verses, joining in
what must have been a very ancient festival,
which is now all but gone. The mood of St
Brigit's day is very different to that of the
lantern festival. The days have just begun to
lengthen after the inwardness of winter, the
earth to breathe out in its great yearly cycle.
That one experience has left me with a
lasting memory that goes beyond my
thinking, conscious self. Some spring
evenings the fading light, or the distant
sound of a child's cry, or the smell of
burning turf will bring me right back to that
February evening in Connemara. Thus we
are deeply affected and formed by the real,
concrete facts of life when we create these
festivals for ourselves and our children.

Pearse O'Shiel, Irish Steiner Waldorf
Early Childhood Association

Why celebrate festivals?

We are creatures of rhythm. Each moment we breathe in and out and the blood pulses through our veins. Each day we awaken from sleep, carry out our day's business and sleep again at night. Over twenty-four hours the sun rises slowly to its height and slowly fades again. Over the course of a year the sun makes this journey 365 times, varying its length, giving us the seasons, with their changing hours of light and warmth, darkness and cold. Deprived of these rhythms we lose a little of ourselves.

It is only within the last 50 years that electricity came to the rural west of Ireland. When a rural society changes so quickly it is all too easy for something to get lost along the way. Double-glazing, insulation, electric light and central heating have made our homes and work places more comfortable, but in doing so have distanced us from the changing seasons. Despite all our time and energy-saving devices we still struggle to fit in all we have to do. At the birth of a friend's child last year, I heard the midwife 'mourning the daffodils', regretting that she had been too busy to notice the daffodils were in bloom until she saw them wilting. Many of us have artificial rhythms imposed upon us by the work we do. As we become more disconnected from the world of nature, we begin to treat nature as a consumable commodity, or disregard it altogether, creating a virtual reality world indoors, inside our heads. There's something unhealthy about this introspection.

Even though we have the ability to divorce ourselves from nature, we need to remember we are still a part of it. It's still important to acknowledge our connection, our place in the ecological circle. The image of the Celtic Cross comes to mind – each point connected, each a part of the whole.

If we take a step back from the edge of the precipice we are currently facing, we can find that celebrating the festivals, the turning points of the year, can restore to us a sense of connection with a greater whole. This requires time: to anticipate and experience the festivals, to notice the changes in the outer environment and the corresponding changes within ourselves.

This book draws heavily on traditional ways that the Irish people have celebrated their festivals in the past. But my intention is not to romanticise the past nor pull us backward in time. Those days are gone and we are not those people. We need new ways to celebrate and connect with the changing seasons. Instead I wanted to offer a healthy mixture of old and new, tradition and innovation through which we can create meaningful celebrations for ourselves within the context of our lives and conditions today. We cannot return to a rural idyll, but we can choose to move forwards with grace.

Ruth Marshall, 2003

Beannachtaí na bhFéile oraibh

(Blessings of the festivals upon you)

Introduction

Before we begin...

Below are a few preparatory, practical suggestions and tips to help nourish and enliven your journey through the Irish year.

About the recipes

Most of the recipes included within the festival calendar are traditional. Some, such as the cashew nut loaf, are given as a vegetarian alternative, while others are simply new ideas that seem appropriate additions. I suggest using wholemeal flour rather than white, using foods as fresh as possible and buying locally grown produce.

If you can, buy certified organic or Demeter (biodynamically grown) products, which contain more life force nourishment as well as vitamins and minerals. Better still, grow your own. Allergy sufferers may wish to substitute goat's-, rice- or soya milk for milk in the recipes.

For the main part recipe ingredients are given in pounds and ounces. Please consult the charts in Appendix 1 for conversion to metric weights.

A festival crafts box

It is a good idea to have a special box or basket stocked with materials ready for making any of the festival crafts. When we celebrate Irish festivals with children we can enrich our lives at no great expense. Many of the suggested crafts use readily available natural materials such as rushes, or can be made from scraps of fabric or wool. See Appendix 1 for suggestions for a well-stocked crafts box.

Festival table

You may also want to designate a special table, shelf or corner of a room as a festival table. The festival table is a special place for displaying seasonal crafts and natural objects. You can spread a coloured cloth to match the mood of the festival. For example, in spring you might use a white, yellow or light green cloth; in summer, lilac, pink, light blue or pale yellow; in autumn you might choose a red, gold, rust or wine coloured cloth, while royal blue or violet might suit the winter.

As well as cloths, you will need a vase or bowl to hold flowers, branches or bare twigs, as appropriate. Again, no great expense is necessary – a few wild flowers arranged with love in a jam jar may be all that is needed to carry the mood of the season.

A Little Myth and History

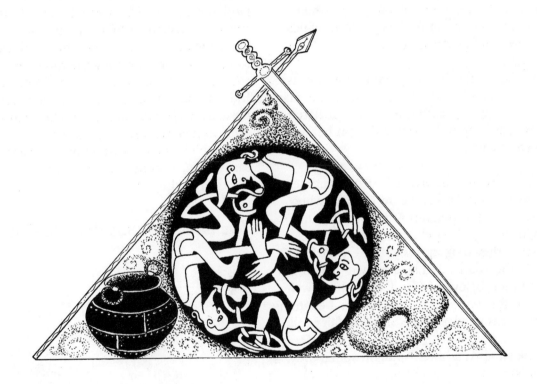

In the 'Book of Invasions' *(Lebor Gabala Erenn)* six races are recalled as arriving in Ireland in the mythic past. The first of these were the people of Cessair, granddaughter of Noah, who came with 30 others in three boats. Next came the company of Parthalon, who made great changes to the land and who all died of plague. The Nemedians were followed by the Fir Bolg ('men of the bag') and then the Tuatha de Danaan – people of Danu, or people skilled in the arts. The sixth of these races were the Milesians, ancestors of the present day Gaels of Ireland and Scotland.

1

The Tuatha de Danaan are perhaps the best remembered in the great tales. When they arrived in Ireland they burned their boats so that they could make no attempt to return. The smoke covered the sun for three days and nights.

They brought with them four treasures: the Stone of Destiny which called out at the touch of the true king; the invincible spear of Lugh; the sword of Nuada from which no one could escape once it was unsheathed; and the cauldron of the Dagda from which no one would leave hungry.

The Tuatha fought two great battles against the Fir Bolgs and the Fomorians on the plain of Moytura. Thereafter peace was declared 'from earth up to heaven and from heaven down to earth'.

The Milesians, children of Scota, daughter of Pharoh faced the Tuatha de Danaan when they arrived in Ireland. After a confrontation, when the mystic poet Amergin spoke (see below), they took up residence on the land, while the Tuatha de Danaan, who would not leave their beloved Ireland, agreed to dwell within the land, in the hollow hills, becoming afterwards known as the Sidhe or fairy folk.

As he stepped ashore, Amergin spoke these words:

I am the wind that breathes upon the sea,
I am a wave of the ocean …
I am a ray of the sun,
I am the most fair of herbs,
I am a wild boar in valour,
I am a salmon in the water,
I am a lake upon a plain,
I am a word of science,
I am the point of a lance in battle,
I am the god who creates fire in the head …

In Irish mythology gods, heroes and landscape are continuously interwoven like the interlace patterns in Celtic art.

The Druids were wise and gifted spiritual advisors of the people. Learned in the arts and science of healing, poetry, vision, law-giving, agriculture, battle-strategy and peace-making, they had a deep understanding of the elements and held in memory a vast store of tales containing the history of their land and people. Many see the druids as spiritual ancestors of Christianity, seeking to live a life of balance, in harmony with the forces of nature, awaiting the foreseen coming of Christ as King of the Elements. Indeed, many tales of Celtic saints portray these as possessing druidic qualities and skills of healing, prophecy and the arts. This may explain why Christianity took root so easily here, as continuation of an older mystical tradition.

The land of saints and scholars

The early Christian saints were the ones who first wrote down the stories and legends of old Ireland. Throughout the 5th to 13th centuries, scholars from Ireland brought learning and the Celtic Christian message to continental Europe and (with St Brendan) America. In monastic communities in Ireland they applied themselves to recording the ancient tales of the Irish people and writing the gospels in beautifully illustrated books such as the Book of Kells. In Ireland a light was kept aflame that was engulfed by wandering hordes in Europe.

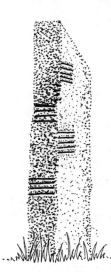

Prior to this the old Ogham (pronounced ohm) script was used as an aide-mémoire. Based on the characters of trees, each letter had a corresponding association. Ogham was carved on stone or wood, or could be signalled using the fingers, which proved useful in communities that had chosen to live in silence.

A few Celtic saints

In Down three saints one grave do fill,

Brigit, Patrick and Colmcille.

Brigit and Patrick have feast days of their own, which are covered in the festival calendar. **Brigit** – see Imbolc, 1 February. **Patrick** – see 17 March.

Colmcille

Colmcille was born in 521 CE of a noble family. (CE – Christian Era, also known as AD or Anno Domini.) His original name, Criomthan, meant Fox. As a prince he was educated by druids and later entered religious life under St Finnian of Moville and later St Finnian of Clonard. When he copied a manuscript of St Finnian's this led to the first recorded copyright case in Ireland. The ruling, that went against Colmcille, stated: 'To every cow her calf, and to every book its little book.' This led to the battle of Culdrevney. As a result, Colmcille left Ireland in exile, vowing not to return until he had saved as many souls as he had caused to be lost in that terrible battle. So in 563 at the age of 42, he sailed towards Scotland. Caught in the Corryvrekin whirlpool, he saved the lives of his crew by throwing into the waters a little soil from the grave of St Ciarán of Clonmacnoise.

He went on to found a community on the island of Iona, from where he brought Christianity to much of Scotland. His was the first recorded encounter with the Loch Ness monster. Colmcille made many prophecies, one of which tells of a new Ireland, 'Eire the prosperous. Great shall be her renown and her might, there shall not be on the surface of this wide earth a land found to equal this fine country.' We live in hope!

Kevin

Feast – 3 June. Born 498. Kevin wished for a life of quiet contemplation, and built a hermitage at Glendalough. Beloved by animals, he stood silent in prayer with both arms outstretched until birds nested upon his hands.

Ciarán

Feast 9 September. Born 514 in County Roscommon, Ciarán was educated by St Finian of Clonard. After seven years with St Enda on the Aran Islands, he spent seven years on an island in Lough Ree and then established a community at Clonmacnoise on the banks of the River Shannon. It was here that the Book of the Dun Cow was written. He was known for his generosity and goodness, so much so that many of the other saints were jealous of him! He died of the yellow plague in 549, aged only 33. Soil from Ciarán's grave is still thought to offer protection to those travelling by water.

Ita

Feast day 15 January. Born in Waterford around 480, she had the gifts of healing and prophecy and a great love for children. She established a monastery on Slaibh Luachra. Known as 'Foster mother of the saints', Ita ran a school for boys and treated each one as she would the Christ child. She wrote, 'The fosterage of my house is not of any common child; Jesus with his heavenly company shelter each night against my heart.' She is associated with Tobernamolt near Ardfert, County Kerry, where St Brendan was baptised. St Ita's Well at Killeedy, County Limerick, stands near her grave. She died around 570.

Gobnait

Feast 11 February. An angel told the young Gobnait that she should leave home and build a monastery where she saw nine white deer. She established many small communities, but at Ballyvourney in County Cork she saw the nine white deer and founded her main community there. A renowned beekeeper, Gobnait saved her people by releasing angry bees to sting attackers.

Brendan

Feast 16 May. Born around 483, educated by Saints Ita and Finian of Clonard. Brendan had a pioneering spirit. He learned from Mayo fishermen of a great land to the West and so he set sail from Dingle, County Kerry, in a little skin boat or currach with the stars as his guide. Seven years later he returned (some say that he had reached America) full of tales and established a community at Clonfert in County Galway, where he was buried in 577 aged 94.

Vikings

During the age of the monasteries, Vikings arrived in search of land and plunder. Scholars and saints alike were put to the sword, churches looted and works of art were destroyed or stolen as booty. The Irish, a collection of tribes under their own leaders, were unable to mass a united defence against the invaders until, one thousand years ago, a tribal chief Brian Boru, a tribal king in Munster, took up the challenge and united the Irish as their High King. In a decisive battle at Clontarf, the Vikings were defeated.

Normans

In 1169 Dermot MacMurrough, king of Leinster offered Irish lands to Norman lords from England for support in retaining his kingdom. He gave his daughter Aoife in marriage to a Norman, Richard de Clare, known as 'Strongbow'. England's King Henry II, concerned that Strongbow and other lords were becoming too powerful, came to Ireland and was declared 'Lord of Ireland' by English lords and many of the Irish kings. Under

Norman rule, towns with stout stone walls grew where there had been Viking trading settlements. Normans settled and often became 'more Irish than the Irish'. Castles and churches were built throughout the land and feudalism, a hierarchical system of government with the king at its head and peasants at the bottom, was established.

Reformation

The Reformation spread throughout Europe in response to corruption and abuse of wealth within the Roman church.

In 1534 England's king Henry VIII broke with Rome and declared himself head of the Church of England, and later of the Church of Ireland. Monasteries were dissolved and their wealth transferred to the English monarch. In areas ruled by the Gaelic Irish little changed as only those loyal to the English crown adopted this reformed church.

A rebellion of the Ulster Irish ended in defeat at the Battle of Kinsale after which the Irish nobles fled the country.

The Plantation of Ulster began in 1609 with lands granted to Scottish nobles who brought over thousands of Scots as tenants. While English planters were largely Anglican, the Scots brought Presbyterianism to the north. Then in 1649 Oliver Cromwell's Roundheads beat the Irish into submission and imposed another plantation.

Plantations

In the 16th century, powerful Irish families who rebelled against English rule had their lands confiscated and granted to settlers loyal to the Crown, known as 'Planters'. Munster, Leinster and Connaught were now largely under English control, while Ulster remained a stronghold of the native Irish.

Catholics who refused to swear allegiance to the Parliament had their lands confiscated and were given the option of going 'To Hell or to Connaught'. Many chose to settle on the poor land west of the Shannon.

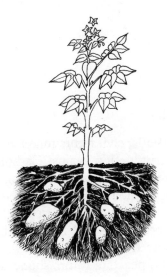

The new Protestant ascendancy introduced new farming methods, and the potato, which happened to grow well on poor land.

At the battle of the Boyne (1690), Irish Catholics supported the army of King James II of England and Protestants supported King William of Orange, a reflection of the political and religious polarisation within Europe at the time.

William's victory meant that Protestant forces ruled in Ireland. Penal Laws prevented Catholics from enjoying an education, owning property or celebrating mass. Catholics continued to practise their outlawed religion, holding masses on mountainsides and at Mass Rocks.

Eventually in 1829 a Catholic Emancipation act gave wealthy Catholics the right to vote.

The Great Hunger

In 1845–1848 a fungal blight struck the potato harvest. The area worst hit was the rural west where potatoes were the staple food crop of the people. This was also the area where Irish language and culture were strongest. The British, with their 'laissez faire' policy, did nothing to relieve the situation until it was well advanced. Approximately two million people died during the Famine and many who survived emigrated to America on 'coffin ships'. The Great Hunger, with its loss of lives and culture, left a deep wound in the Irish psyche.

Independence

In 1916 nationalist feeling within Ireland led to the Easter Rising, followed by the formation of Dáil Éireann and later the birth of the Republic of Ireland. With Partition the country was divided into north (British) and south (Irish Free State).

The descendants of the Scottish Protestant settlers in the north preferred to remain part of the United Kingdom, loyal to the Crown, hence the names 'Unionist' and 'Loyalist'. Politics and religion are closely entwined, particularly in Northern Ireland.

The Troubles

In the late 1960s, civil rights marches brought discrimination against Catholics in Northern Ireland in terms of housing and employment to the public eye. Peaceful protests were followed by outbreaks of violence on both sides that have continued since. With the IRA ceasefire in 1994 the possibility of a peaceful future shone through.

However, even today the situation in the North is still unsettled. While the news still carries stories of sectarian violence, many ordinary people as well as politicians, on both sides of the cultural divide, continue to work for peace and reconciliation.

The Year's Turning – The Wheel of the Celtic Year

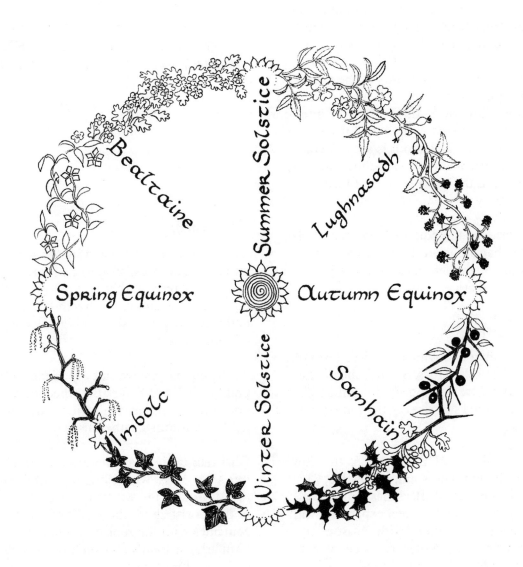

If we watch the movement of the sun, moon and stars over the course of a year, we can begin to imagine how ancient peoples saw time as a wheel constantly turning. The sun and moon were seen to gather strength and die away again as they encircled the heavens.

The sun cross

The ancient inhabitants of Ireland honoured and recorded the movements of the sun in the construction of stone circles and megalithic monuments, like Newgrange in the Boyne Valley, Co. Meath, whose central chamber the midwinter sun illuminates as it rises.

The four major solar events of the year – winter and summer solstices and spring and autumn equinoxes – divide the year into four quarters, expressed as an equal-armed cross within a circle. This motif is seen in gold sun-disk ornaments from the megalithic age and later in the stone crosses of Celtic Christianity.

The solstices and equinoxes are fixed solar events that occur on the same days each year, although their exact times can be found in a good diary or almanac.

The solstices

The summer and winter solstices form one axis of the solar cross. Solstice means the time when the sun appears to stand still. For three days the sun rises at the same point on the horizon.

Winter solstice, 21 December, is the shortest day of the year and summer solstice, 21 June, is the longest. Each has a different quality: in summer we feel expanded, with our energies 'out there' with blossoming nature, while the winter draws us inward searching for light within. Modern science

acknowledges that we react to differing levels of sunlight, for example, in the diagnosis of SAD (seasonal affective disorder). At the solstices we can benefit from standing still ourselves to review what has changed in us since the previous solar event.

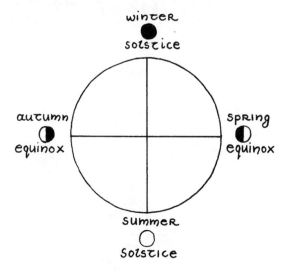

The equinoxes

The second axis is created by the spring and autumn equinoxes, around 21 March and 21 September respectively. At the time of the equinoxes the sun rises directly in the east and sets directly west, creating day and night of equal length.

At the equinoxes, we can experience a brief point of balance before the wheel moves on once more – either into spring's increasing light or autumn's gathering dark.

Christian festivals are superimposed upon this solar cross, with Christmas celebrated just days after the winter solstice. The birth of the Christ child, the 'Light of the world', coincides with the rebirth of the sun. Similarly, St John's Day on 24 June coincides with the summer solstice.

The fire festivals

The Celts divided the year into four quarters, corresponding with the four seasons. The fire festivals of Samhain, Imbolc, Bealtaine, Lughnasadh are the gateways to each season and mark the turning points of the farming and country year. However these festivals are not only agricultural events, they also reflect subtle changes within the energies of the earth and cosmos that affect us all.

One axis of the cross is formed by Bealtaine and Samhain – opposite to each other and dividing the year into two halves: a time of greater sun or summer and a time of lesser sun or winter.

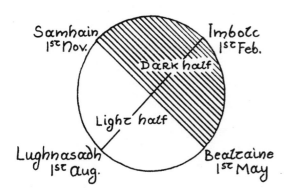

Samhain, 1 November: death and transformation

Samhain marks the beginning of winter and the dark half of the year. Cattle are brought down to lower pastures or indoors, harvest is over, nature sleeps.

Bealtaine, 1 May: fertility

Marks the beginning of summer, the light half of the year. Cattle are brought to the summer pastures.

The festivals of Imbolc and Lughnasadh form the other axis of this cross.

Imbolc, 1 February: renewal

First day of spring, the time when lambs are born.

Lughnasadh, 1 August: harvest

First fruits, beginning of harvest and autumn.

Celebration of each of these fire festivals traditionally begins at dusk on the evening before the feast. The Celtic New Year begins at Samhain, the long dark night before the sun rises to strength again in spring. Although we have given each a fixed date, there is practical sense in the claim that these festivals, as outdoor events, were actually celebrated on the nearest full moon to the first sign of the new season, e.g., for spring, the appearance of the first green shoots.

Superimposed on each other, these two crosses form eight spokes of the year's wheel. This wheel is a powerful symbol seen in the Celtic cross and Brigit's crosses. It is also found in the equal-armed cross cut into the top of each round cake of Irish Soda Bread before it is baked.

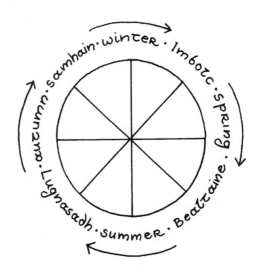

Autumn to Winter

Samhain

Samhain, 31 October
(pronounced sauwain)

Also known as Hallowe'en, Snap Apple Night, Hollantide, Púca Night, Oíche na Sprideanna, Oíche na Cleas (night of the tricks)

The Celtic year begins, as life begins, in darkness, in the womb that is also a tomb. According to Roman authors, the druids believed that 'souls do not die but after death pass into other bodies'. This belief in reincarnation was so strong that a debt unsettled at the time of death could be carried over to the next life! Samhain, a time when plants die back and nature no longer embraces us, is when people remember the dead and the worlds beyond this world.

Samhain is a three-day festival that encompasses Hallowe'en, All Saints' and All Souls' Days. It is a threshold time, marking the end of the bright days of summer and the beginning of the dark half of the year. At such threshold times, the veil between worlds is thin. This means that the beings that inhabit the Otherworld can walk among mortals. A gate is open through which a family's beloved dead can revisit the familiar places and people of their earthly lives. The Sídhe, also known as the Fairies, the Good Folk, Little People or Tuatha De Danann, move from their summer residence to their winter quarters. They can be seen riding in procession from one *rath* (fairy fort) to another across the land. It is traditional to put out a bowl of milk or porridge or a piece of cake for the fairies as they pass by your house.

All crops had to be gathered in before Samhain and no berries could be picked after this time, as the Pooka would spit on them. The last sheaf of the harvest left standing in the field was named the *Cailleach* or Hag. This 'old woman', who was formerly revered

as the crone aspect of the Celtic triple goddess (maiden: Brigit; mother: Macha; crone: Morrigan) has since dwindled into the figure of the witch, dressed in black with cauldron and broomstick. Weather forecasts for the winter were made according to the direction and strength of the wind at midnight on Hallowe'en or by the movement of clouds over the moon.

A simple cross of wood bound with straw, the *parshell*, was made and placed above the door of the house to ensure good fortune. Cattle that could not be fed over the winter were slaughtered. This meant there was plenty of fresh food for a celebration feast. The excess was preserved for the cold winter months ahead by salting or smoking. The bones were burnt on a bonfire (or bone-fire) along with all the impurities of the past six months, since the Bealtaine fires. Even today there is still a great thrill to be had in sitting by a bonfire on a winter night, wrapped in a blanket, holding a turnip lantern against the dark and sharing ghost stories.

People dressed up in suits and masks made of straw or other disguises and went visiting their neighbours at Hallowe'en. In parts of County Cork there was a procession led by a hobby horse called the Láir Bhan (white mare). On Inis Mór, in the Aran Islands, adults in fancy dress today still walk from house to house, without speaking (for that would reveal their identity) and enjoy the hospitality of their neighbours. Elsewhere, it is mainly children who go 'guising'. They walk the streets wearing masks, or with painted faces, carrying turnip lanterns, torches and bags full of goodies, looking like little ghosts and witches as they go trick-or-treating from house to house, gathering sweets, fruit, nuts and money.

While the veil between the worlds of the living and the spirits is thin, information was received from sympathetic ancestral spirits as to how the family would fare in the year ahead. Some people melted scraps of lead in a tablespoon and poured this through a key into a basin of cold water. The shapes formed by the solidifying metal were interpreted as portents for the year ahead. Many divination rituals are still performed, but as fortune-telling games at Hallowe'en parties. Their ripples can be seen in the Hallowe'en Breac – a cake containing a gold ring and other tokens, which would tell who could expect to be married and who would remain a bachelor or spinster.

*A*S SUMMER *turned to autumn we stored the best apples for Hallowe'en, or Snap Apple Night as we called it. We diligently watched the nut trees, hoping that they would be ripe in time, but ripe or not we always picked them. These trees were tall with high, arching branches far from the ground, so it took all our climbing skills to conquer them. We climbed to the top and then as far out along the swaying branches as we dared, while we swung up and down at precarious angles, grasping bunches of nuts and throwing them down to the collector on the ground. Finally, gallons full, we slithered to the ground and danced home through the gathering dusk, scratched but triumphant. That night we cracked our nuts with a stone on the flagstone before the fire while apples swung from cords tied to the meat hooks on the rafters of the kitchen or floated in the timber tub of water in the middle of the floor.*

From *To School Through the Fields*
by Alice Taylor

I have news for you; the stag bells, winter snows, summer is over.
Wind high and cold, the sun low, short its course, the sea running high.
Deep red is the bracken, its shape lost; the wild goose raises its familiar cry.
Cold seizes the bird's wings; season of ice, this is my news.

Irish, 9th century, translated Kuno Meyer, *Early Irish Poetry*

The Adventures of Nera

*I*N *RATH CRUACHAN it was Samhain eve. Queen Maeve and her consort Aileall sat arguing by a roaring fire, as was their way. For sport, Aileall offered a rich reward to any man brave enough to go out into the dark night and tie a withye (or twig) around the leg of a man who had been hanged that day.*

One by one bold warriors strode out into the night to the gallows tree. One by one they crept back into the hall, shaken and pale with fright, for, as you know, at Samhain the spirits of the dead are abroad and the night is full of ghosts. Then Nera stood up calling, 'I will take up this challenge,' and went out into the night with his withye.

'Don't be creeping about, man,' came a voice from the gallows. Nera looked up and the hanged man spoke to him again, 'Here, twist the twig like this and tie it around my ankle.' Nera tied the withye, a little surprised.'That's the way. Now, cut me down from this tree and carry me to yonder cabin. Sure I was dying of thirst before they hanged me, and I need a drink of water before I can rest!'

Nera cut down the hanged man and carried him on his back towards the cabin. As they got closer, he saw a ring of blue flames surrounding it, that seemed to dance up towards the sky.

'Ah now, there's a wise wife that covered the ashes before she went to bed. I'll get no

drink there,' said the hanged man.

A ring of deep water surrounded the next cabin they approached. 'Ah now, these folks have thrown out their dirty water before they went to bed. I'll get no drink there.'

Nera carried the hanged man to a third house. No ring of fire or water barred the way and they entered in. Dirty water from the supper dishes sat under a layer of grease. The hanged man drank most of the filthy water from the tub and spat the rest of it over the sleeping family, who blistered under its touch.

'Now carry me back to the gallows, man, and good night to you.'

After setting the dead man back up on the gallows, Nera set off back to Rath Cruachan to claim his reward, but was dismayed at what he saw there. The fortress was aflame and it seemed that all his friends had been slain by the fairy folk from the sídhe.

From behind a tree, Nera watched as the fairy folk returned to their sídhe mound, and slipped in behind them before the entrance disappeared. The fairy guards stopped him and brought him before the king, who greeted him warmly. The fairy king gave Nera his beautiful daughter as a bride, and ordered a mighty feast. There were the most heavenly wines in the finest of crystal goblets. There were lobsters and hams and sides of beef on golden platters. There were mushrooms and carrots and potatoes in gravy. There were candied fruits and sugared violets, and many more wonders besides. The feasting and the dancing went on for weeks.

Nera was besotted with his lovely bride, and he wanted for nought in the land of the sídhe, where the weather was always fine and the people beautiful. His happiness was complete when his wife gave birth to a lovely boy with Nera's dark hair, and her own bright blue eyes.

There was a well within the sídhe. Nera saw that each day a blind man came to the well, carrying a lame man on his back. Each day the blind man asked, 'Is it there?' and when the lame man replied, 'It is there,' the pair would go off again.

Puzzled by this, Nera asked his wife what it meant. She explained, 'The two are guardians of the king's crown and treasures that lie hidden within the well. The blind man can't see it and the lame man can't run away with it.'

She also told him that Rath Cruachan still stood and all his friends were still alive, that the fire and destruction had been only an illusion.

'My love, I overheard my father, the king, say that he will ride against Rath Cruachan next Samhain. You must return to the world of men and warn them. They must attack the sídhe

before the people of the sídhe destroy them! Here, take these fresh strawberries with you, that they may know you come from the Otherworld. Only promise me that you will come for me, and our child, when Aileall comes to battle with the Sídhe.'

'I will return for you, dearest one.'

With a basket of luscious summer fruits in his hand, Nera walked through the golden gates of the Sídhe. On the path to Rath Cruachan he shivered, for winter was approaching fast in the land of mortal men. He warned Maeve and Aileall of the planned attack, showing the summer fruits to any who doubted where he had been all this past year. They gathered their warriors and prepared for battle. In vain Queen Maeve tried to persuade Nera to stay and fight with them, for he was known as a great hero.

As he had promised, Nera brought his wife and child to safety while Aileall's army attacked the sídhe and plundered its treasure. When all was over, Nera returned with his family and all their cattle and goods to the land of perpetual summer, to make their home once more within the sídhe. And never was he seen again in the land of men.

*I*N THE BROWN DAYS *of early October, the dying
year brought us a new bounty. As soon as the
word was out, we emptied the books out of our
satchels and headed to Carnacrow Wood to pick
nuts. The hazel woods were full of colour, the
leaves were golden and brown and russet and
the sun shone into little clearings where some of
the nuts had shelled and fallen on the matted
ground.*

*We picked the shiny shelled ones from the
mossy ground and then we climbed into the
branches for the nuts that still wore their half-
tunic of green. If they shelled easily they were
ripe; if their coats were obstinate they were
unripe. We pulled them anyway, regardless of
their readiness.*

*This was one of days of plenty; we might
never be here again. The world might come to
an end, or we might die, never knowing the
sweetness of the sin of gluttony.*

*We sat on the rocks under the whispering
hazel and broke the nuts open with stones. You
had to be skilful: too hard a blow made
everything mush, and you had to pick out
splinters of shell. Some of the older boys could
crack the nuts in their teeth and spit out the
shells through the air with a 'thup' sound of the
tongue.*

*Some kernels were sweet as honey; some
were raw as a cabbage stalk. It didn't matter.
We ate them all regardless, old and new, sweet
and sour. We filled our satchels and brought
them home. We broke them open on the stone
floor with the smoothing-iron. Walking across
the kitchen then in your bare feet was a
hazardous journey: you could find a sharp shell
under your heel.*

*We always vowed to keep a store of nuts for
another Hallowe'en, but that seldom worked out.*

From *Once in a Green Summer*
by Thomas F. Walsh

Festive food

*Did you ever eat colcannon
when 'twas made with yellow cream
And the kale and praties blended
like a picture in a dream?*

*Did you ever scoop a hole on top
to hold the melting lake
Of the clover-flavoured butter
which your mother used to make?*

*Ah God be with the happy days
when troubles we had not
And our mothers made colcannon
in the little skillet pot.*

Praties – potatoes
Colcannon – a dish made from cooked
    cabbage or kale with potatoes mashed
    together with onions
Skillet – a large round pot with three little
    feet and two handles)

Colcannon

Ingredients:
1 lb / 450g kale or cabbage
2 cups water
1 tbsp olive oil
1 lb / 450g potatoes, peeled and quartered
1 cup chopped leeks
1 cup milk
2 oz / 50g melted butter
salt and pepper
1 tbsp chopped parsley

Method:
Cook, drain and mash the potatoes.
Simmer the kale or cabbage with the olive oil in 2 cups water for 10 minutes. Drain and chop finely.
Simmer the leeks in the milk for 10 minutes.
Add the chopped kale or cabbage, leeks and milk to the mashed potato and stir well.
Add salt and pepper to taste.
Form the mixture into a mound on a large plate and pour over the melted butter.
Garnish with parsley.

Boxty on the griddle

Ingredients:
1 lb / 450g flour
1 tsp baking soda
1 lb / 450g raw potatoes
1 lb / 450g cooked mashed potato
buttermilk to mix

Method:
Peel and grate the raw potatoes. Squeeze the grated potatoes in a tea towel to extract all the juices. Leave the liquid to settle in a bowl.
Mix the grated potato into the mashed potato. Add the starch from the potato water, the flour, baking soda and mix well.

Add enough buttermilk to form a dropping consistency. Beat well and leave to stand for a few minutes.
Fry spoonfuls of the batter in a greased heavy pan or griddle, turning so that both sides are cooked.

Boxty on the griddle, boxty on the pan
If you don't eat boxty, you'll never get a man.

Fadge

Ingredients:
Apples
4 oz / 110g flour
1 lb / 450g potatoes
1/2 tsp salt
1 oz / 25g butter
Sugar to taste

Method:
Peel, boil and mash the potatoes. Mix in the flour until you have a pliable dough.
On a floured surface, roll out the dough into two equal sized rounds.
Cut the apples into thick slices and lay them on one round. Cover with the other round and pinch the edges to seal.
Cook on a griddle (or in the oven) until both sides are cooked and the apples are soft inside.
Slice around the edges and peel back the top layer. Add butter and sugar and cover with the lid.
Leave in a warm place until the butter and sugar melt to form a sauce.
Cut into slices and eat while it's hot.

Hallowe'en Breac

Ingredients:
1 lb / 450g flour
2 oz / 50g butter
8 oz / 225g sultanas
8 oz / 225g currants
1 tsp dried yeast
1/2 pint / 275ml milk, warmed
2 oz / 50g sugar
4 oz / 110g mixed peel
1 tsp ground cinnamon
Pinch nutmeg
Pinch salt
2 eggs, beaten
A ring wrapped in greaseproof paper (you might also include a dried pea, dried bean)

Method:
Add the yeast and half the sugar to the warm milk and leave to sit in a warm place.
Sift the flour together with the salt and spices into a large bowl, then rub in the butter. Mix in the rest of the sugar.
Add the warmed milk and yeast mixture and the beaten eggs, and beat well. Fold in the fruit and peel and the trinkets.
Turn the mixture into a greased and lined 8-inch (20cm) cake tin. Cover with a tea towel and leave in a warm place to rise until it has doubled in size. Bake in a hot oven for one hour.

When the cake is sliced, everyone hopes to get the slice with the ring. The ring indicates a wedding; the pea – poverty; the bean – riches.

Garlic honey syrup

This is an old herbal remedy, useful for colds and coughs.

Ingredients:
Cloves of garlic
Clear honey

Method:
Peel the garlic cloves. Crush them in a jam jar and cover them with clear runny honey.
Stir the mixture, cover it and then leave it to sit.

This can be taken by the spoonful fresh from the jar, or you can strain and bottle it. It will keep for years.

Games

Most of the traditional Hallowe'en games originated as divination rites, and most of these are to do with finding the identity of one's future love.

Nutshells

Sitting by an open fire, place two hazelnuts, or two dried beans side by side on the grate or in the ashes. Give the pair the names of a courting couple, e.g. John and Mary. Watch to see what happens to the pair when they react to the warmth of the fire.

If the two nuts stay together it bodes well for the couple.
If they burst into flames, it suggests a passionate future.
If the two jump apart, this couple will part soon.

Spell to reveal a true love's name

A girl wishing to know the name and profession of her true love cuts nine stalks of yarrow with a black-handled knife. She remains silent from suppertime until bedtime. Then she peels the yarrow stalks, while speaking this verse:

Good morrow, good morrow, my pretty yarrow
I pray before this time tomorrow
You'll tell me who my true love shall be.
The clothes he wears, the name he bears
And the day that he'll come to wed me.

She can then expect to see her true love in a dream.

Snap-apple

This game was played with a cross of wood suspended by a string from a rafter beam. On two ends of the cross were rosy apples. On the other two ends were lighted candles. The whole thing was spun around and players would leap up to try and bite the apple – without being burnt by the candles. This game may have originated from a kind of trial by fire. A safer version can be played with unwashed potatoes instead of candles.

You will need:
2 sticks about 45cm / 18 inches in length
2 apples
2 unwashed potatoes

Method:
Take two sticks about 45cm / 18 inches long and sharpen both their ends to points. Fasten them together crosswise with wire or string.
Suspend from a hook in the ceiling by a string. Stick apples onto two of the points and potatoes on the other two.
The whole thing is spun around. Each player in turn tries to take a bite out of the apple.

As you can imagine, sometimes you get a mouthful of potato!

Bobbing for apples

This game has its origins in trials by water.

You will need:
A basin or bucket filled with water
Waterproof sheet or newspapers
Red apples

Method:
Fill a basin (a baby-bath is a good size) with water and place it on the floor.
It's a good idea to put this on newspapers or a waterproof sheet, as there will undoubtedly be splashes.
Add some red apples, which float about on the surface of the water.

To play:
Players stand in line. Each in turn gets down on his★ knees on the floor beside the basin.
With hands tied behind his back, he must try to catch an apple with his mouth. This is more difficult than it sounds, as the apples begin to sink as soon as you touch them! Whoever catches an apple can eat it!

You can make this trial by water more challenging by tossing in a few silver coins. These will sink to the bottom of the basin. Players have to put their faces right under the water to pick these up in their teeth.

Alternatively, the players stand over the basin with a fork held in their teeth. At a given signal they try to fork apples out of the basin. The player can eat any apples speared.

* To avoid the awkward use of 'he or she' each time, I will alternate gender from game to game – the author

Fortune-telling

You will need:
4 plates or bowls
Water, flour, clay and a ring

Method:
Four plates are laid on the table. One plate contains water, another holds a ring, one holds clay and the fourth holds flour.
Players are blindfolded and led to the table. The four plates are rearranged each time, so that no one knows which lies where.
The player's fortune for the coming year is told according to which plate she places her hand upon.

Water foretells a journey; the ring foretells love; clay foretells a death and the flour, wealth.

Dead Man Arise

This is a chase game, not a traditional Samhain game, but it would be quite appropriate to play it at a Hallowe'en party.

One player lies on the floor, buried under a pile of blankets or coats.
The other players walk slowly around him in a circle, solemnly chanting, 'Dead man arise, dead man arise, dead man arise'.

Then, when they least expect it, the 'dead man' leaps up and chases them. The first to be caught becomes the next 'dead man' and the game continues.

Tir na Nog

This game is played out of doors in the dark. Any number can play. You need a long quiet stretch of driveway, track or unused road where there will be no traffic.

To play:
A spot is chosen and identified as the den or Tir na Nog.
One player is chosen to be the Guardian of the Entrance to Tir na Nog. He sits or stands in the middle of the road with eyes closed and a torch in his hand.
The other players line up together, facing the Guardian, but about 4.5m / 15 feet away. The players try to sneak past the Guardian to Tir na Nog.
If the Guardian hears any movement or rustling, he shines his torch in that direction. Anyone caught in the light must stop and freeze.
When most players are frozen, you can call a truce and let them begin again from the starting line.
The first player to sneak past the Guardian and reach the entrance to Tir na Nog becomes the new Guardian, and the game continues.

Green Gravel

Green Gravel

Green gravel, green gravel, your grass is so green. You're the
fair-est young damsel that e-ver was seen.

This old Belfast street game portrays the preparations for a funeral.

To play:
The players form a ring, holding hands and walk around singing this song:

Green gravel, green gravel,
*   your grass is so green,*
You're the fairest young damsel
*   that ever was seen.*

We washed her, we dressed her,
*   we rolled her in silk,*
And we wrote down her name
*   with a glass pen and ink.*

Dear Annie, dear Annie,
*   your true love is dead,*
And we send you a letter
*   to turn round your head.*

After the song is finished, the child whose name was spoken in the second last line (in this example Annie) turns around so that she faces out of the ring. She joins hands with the players on either side of her and the game continues until another child's name is spoken. This child also turns to face out of the circle.
The game continues until the whole circle is facing outwards.

Black Magic

This is an indoor party game. Two players who know the game claim that one of them is a mind reader, and the other her charming assistant.

To play:
The mind reader leaves the room and the assistant selects an object that can be seen in the room, with the help of the others present. For example: 'This blue cushion.'
Once an object has been selected the mind reader is invited back in.
The assistant points to various objects and asks the mind reader, 'Is this it?' The mind reader is able to correctly identify the chosen object every time, to the amazement of the audience, who are left trying to figure out how it's done!

How does it work? The assistant points to the selected object immediately after he has pointed to or spoken about something that is black – hence the name – Black Magic!

Things to make and do

Turnip lantern

You will need:
A turnip (you can also use a pumpkin, sugar
  beet or other vegetable)
A large sharp knife
Small pointed knife
Apple corer
Tablespoon
A candle or nightlight
Knitting needle
String or wire

Method:
With a large, sharp knife, cut off the top of
  the turnip. Do this as neatly as possible,
  because this will become the lid of your
  lantern.
To hollow the turnip, use the apple corer and
  a smaller knife to loosen the pulp. Remove
  the pulp with the tablespoon.
Once the middle has been removed work
  more cautiously, removing smaller pieces
  until the walls of the turnip are uniformly
  thick and there is a flat spot at the base in
  which to place a candle.

From the outside cut holes for eyes, nose
  and mouth to make a face for your turnip
  lantern. This can be as friendly or as
  gruesome as you wish!
With a knitting needle make two holes at
  either side of the lantern. Thread the
  string or wire through the holes and knot
  it to make a carrying handle.
Place a candle or nightlight inside the
  lantern.
Now hollow out the lid in the same way,
  cutting holes to allow smoke out. Replace
  the lid.

You can carry the lantern by the string or
suspend the string from a stick. Carry it with
you as you visit your neighbours at
Hallowe'en.

Now that pumpkins are available in the
shops at Hallowe'en, you may find that they
are much easier to hollow out than the
traditional turnips.

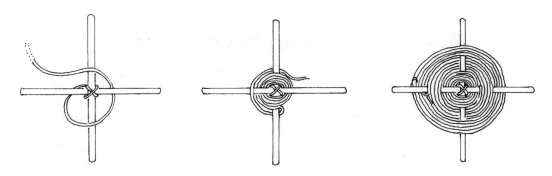

Parshell

You will need:
2 wooden sticks about 18cm / 7 inches long
Fine ribbon or yarn

Method:
Place two sticks together to form a cross.
  Bind them together with the yarn or fine
  ribbon, starting at the crossing point and
  then weaving under one arm, over the
  next in a clockwise direction.
Continue until you have woven about 1.25cm/
  1/2 inch and then change direction,
  weaving over and under anticlockwise for
  another 1.25cm / 1/2 inch.
Continue in this way, changing direction
  after each 1.25cm / 1/2 inch of weaving,
  until only about one inch of the sticks is
  left exposed.
Fasten off the yarn.

In olden times the Parshell was made with
sticks and bound with straw. It was placed
above the doorway inside the house to ward
off ill luck and sickness for the coming year.
A new one would be made to replace the
old Parshell each Hallowe'en.

Make your own broomstick

You too can be the proud owner of a
Nimbus 2002!

You will need:
Birch twigs
Length of ash or hazel
  or a broom handle
Wire or twine

Method:
Gather a bundle of birch twigs. Arrange
  them so that all the thicker ends are
  together.
Bind the twigs tightly at the thick end using
  strong twine or wire.
Use a broom handle or cut a length of hazel
  or ash for a handle. Sharpen one end of
  the handle and push this into the middle
  of the bundle of twigs.
Use your broom to sweep up dead leaves, or
  as part of your Hallowe'en costume.

Casadh Cam na Feadarnai   A traditional song from County Armagh

Ag casadh Cam na Feadarnai
Ar dhul isteach sa tsléibh dhuit
Ar thaobh do láimhe deise dhuit
Tá toigh na Cailli Riabhai

Pronounced:
(ah cassa cam na fadernee)
(ergoll istchallk se shlave gwit)
(er heave daw lawve deshi gwit)
(tawtee na kylie reevie)

> Chorus:
> *With a ma ring a doo a day*
> *With a ma ring a doo a daddio*

Bhí Bunnaidh Chinn is Bannaidh Chinn
Is Neidí beag a' tsléibh' ann
'Sé Velvet bocht a d'ársódh duit
Cá mbíonn an Chailleach Riabhach

(bee bonny hin is banny hin)
(is neddy beg a shlave an)
(shay velvet bocht a darsho ditch)
(caw meen an kyla reebach)

> Chorus

Hallowe'en

Oiche roimh mhí Shamhna	(eeha reev ee how nah)
A' tarraingt mhóin a' Tiarna	(a tarrint vone a tirna)
Bhí Neansaí Gabha 's na gasúir	(bi nansi gowsna gassure)
Ag creach na Caillí Riabhai.	(a grack na kylie reevie)

Chorus

Da bhfeicfea Micheál O Báinichinn	(da vecka meelo bannichin)
'S é ag imeacht lena chliabhán	(shay gimmacht lenna cleevon)
A' cruinniú ábhar tine	(a crinnu awver tinna)
Lena 'dandy-cap' a ghrianadh.	(Linn a dandy-cap a greena)

Chorus

The song translates roughly as follows:

The Double bend at Feadarnach

At the double bend at Feadarnach, as you go into the mountain, on your right hand side is the house of the Brindled Hag.

Bunnaidh Chinn and Bannaidh Chinn were there, and little Ned from the mountain. It's poor Velvet who would relate to you where the Brindled Hag is.

The night before November, drawing the landlord's turf, the Blacksmith's Nancy and the lads were at the plundering of the Brindled Hag.

There was Micheal O Bainichinn going off with his creel, gathering fuel for the fire to sun his dandy cap.

All Saints' Day, 1 November
All Souls' Day, 2 November

Continuing the practices of the pagan Celts, the Christian church honours the dead on All Saints' and All Souls' days.

People believed that the dead revisited their old homes on the night of 1 November. They must be made welcome, so the door was left unlocked. The table was set with a place for each dead relative and a bowl of fresh spring water. A candle was lit for each deceased and left to burn itself out when the living went to their beds.

On All Souls' Day, people say prayers for the dead, visit family graves, tidy them up and lay fresh flowers there.

Nowadays we might place framed photographs of our ancestors in a prominent place (perhaps, just for today, on the seasonal table). This could be a good time to light a candle for our grandmothers and grandfathers and to share the stories of their lives.

Things to make

Decorative corner for a picture frame

You will need:
Tracing paper
Dark pencil

Method:
Trace the design below and transfer to picture-mount corners.
You can decorate one corner, two diagonally opposite each other, or all four corners.
Colour in the design.

To trace, place tracing paper over the design and trace using a dark pencil. Turn the tracing paper over and place onto the picture mount where you wish to reproduce the design. Go over the lines pressing lightly with your pencil, being careful not to move the paper. The design will now be transferred to the mount.
Turn the tracing paper again and repeat this process to transfer the design to another corner.

Clip frame with Celtic design

You could also paint this corner design onto the glass of a frameless photo frame (clip frame) using glass paints and outliner.

Glass paints are available in many colours in small jars and the outliner comes in a tube with a long nose that can be used like a pen. **Warning:** use in a well-ventilated space.

You will need:
'Clip frame' a little bigger than your photo
Glass paints in two colours
Tube of outliner in gold or silver

Method:
Photocopy the interlace pattern to the size you require.
Placing the photocopy under the glass, trace the outline onto the glass using the outliner. Wait for this to dry thoroughly.
Paint in the colours within the outlines, being careful to follow the line of each strand of the knotwork pattern.
Leave to dry, insert photo and clip frame together.

Celtic knotwork border for a photo or picture frame

You will need:
Pencil
Ruler
Coloured pencils or paints

Method:
1. Mark a border 1.5cm wide on card. The sides of the border must be a whole number in length (i.e. 10cm but not 10.5cm). Draw parallel lines within the border, dividing it into three equal parts (0.5cm) as shown on the next page. You now have four construction lines A, B, C and D. Use your pencil very lightly, as you may wish to erase these lines later.
2. On line B, starting in the corner at point x, mark every cm along the line with a dot. On line C start at point y and mark every cm with a dot.
3. Now join the dots to make a zigzag line all the way round.
4. Join alternate dots between lines AB, creating overlapping curves, as shown. Repeat with alternate dots between lines CD. Leave corner areas empty.
5. There are many ways of creating corners. Here are two – perhaps you can also make up your own, just make sure that all the lines join up in a continuous flow.
   a) Make a diagonal line from corner A to corner D. Continue the border pattern to this line in both directions until they meet. You should now have a mirror image either side of the line. It may need a little adjustment, such as rounding the inner corner.
   b) This is a more challenging corner design. Join the two outer curves along the corner edge. Adjust remaining curves as shown. Make a little picture of your own in the corner space. It may be a detail from the picture you are framing.

6. So far you have been drawing construction lines. Now you are ready for the real thing!

If you are using **corner 5a**, there are five lines or 'ribbons'. Choose a different colour pencil for each ribbon, making sure that you use colour pencils that do not smudge when rubbed with an eraser.
Starting at the top left hand corner on line A, begin to colour the line, thickening it a little, until you reach the first line that crosses your ribbon. Leave a gap and continue so that it appears that your ribbon goes under the line. When you reach the next line, your ribbon goes over the line.
Continue in this way going under, over, under, over the lines until you have created a ribbon all the way round the border.
Now start with the next colour on corner B. This time your ribbon goes over the first line and under the next. Continue until that ribbon is completed. Now start at corner C with a new colour. This ribbon goes under then over.
The fourth ribbon starts at corner D and goes over, then under. The fifth ribbon rounds the corner of the construction lines but you can start parallel to the other corners. This ribbon goes under, over.

If you are using **corner 5b**, you will need between one and three colours. Start at the top left hand corner, with A going under, over, under, over as above. The next ribbon starts at corner D, going over, under, but it will not go all around the border. It will return at the next corner until you get back to where you began.
Fill in any remaining ribbons. Repeat this process on each side. If you are designing a different corner you may find the variation creates less colours or one continuous ribbon.

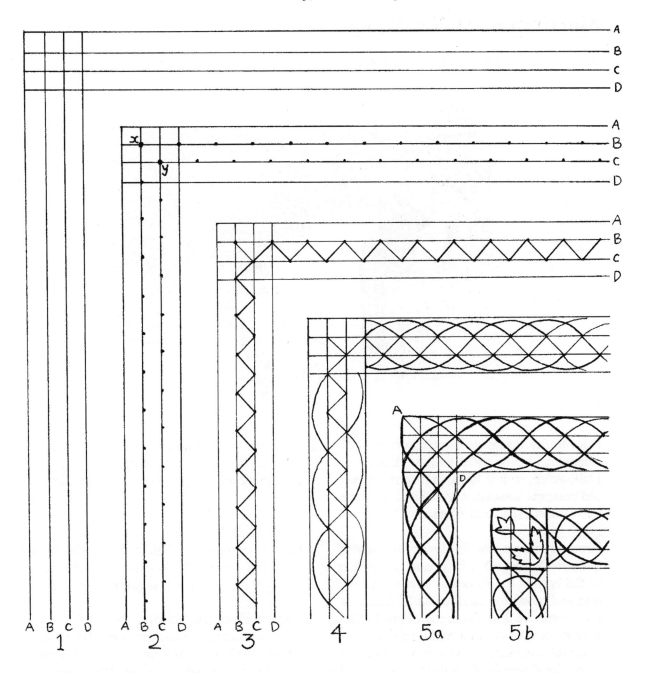

When you have completed the border, erase the construction lines A, B, C and D, being careful not to smudge the colours.

Now you know the secret of the scribes.

You can glue a picture or photograph inside the border or cut out a rectangle or square with a craft knife (with an adult to help), slightly smaller than your picture, and mount it behind.

Martinmas, 11 November

Nine days and a night without counting, from November night to St Martin's Night.

Prior to the change to the Gregorian calendar, 11 November was the date of Hallowe'en, so it is likely that some of the old customs associated with Samhain have been transposed to St Martin's Day.

Some say that it was St Martin who shaved St Patrick's head when he became a monk, and so this is what led Patrick to offer a pig to each nun and monk for sacrifice on St Martin's eve. It may be that this is the origin of the custom of 'Bleeding for St Martin', where a cockerel was killed on Martinmas and a little of its blood sprinkled on the threshold and in the four corners of the house to ensure a prosperous year. The cockerel would then be eaten as part of a Martinmas feast.

Because St Martin is believed to have met his death in a mill wheel, there is a tradition that no work that involved turning a wheel was to

be done on Martinmas. This meant that no meal could be ground, no spinning, no ploughing and no travel, whether by cart or boat.

This is also Armistice Day, a time for remembering those killed in battle during the First and Second World Wars. In Ulster there are local parades to war memorials on this day.

Born in Hungary, Martin (316 – 397 CE) was a soldier in the Roman army. When he met a starving and freezing beggar, Martin took his sword and cut his soldier's cloak in two, giving one half to the beggar. That night he dreamed that Christ came to him, wearing this same cloak. Leaving the Roman army, Martin established a monastery at Marmoutier where 80 or so monks lived in caves carved out of a cliff face, meeting only for prayers and to eat together. This community became a model for western monasticism, and inspired the founding of the earliest Christian churches throughout Ireland, Scotland and Wales, such as Whithorn on the Solway Firth and Nendrum on Island Mahee in Strangford Lough, County Down.

Things to do

The motifs of sacrifice, sharing and giving up the way of the soldier can inspire us to be generous at this time and to focus on peace.

Giveaway

Invite friends to a Martinmas dinner. Ask each guest to bring something with them as a 'giveaway'. This should be a small thing, chosen from amongst their own possessions, something that they really like and that has some special meaning for them. At the meal, each one present gives away an offering in friendship.

Breathing in Peace

Sit in silence for one minute in remembrance of all who have lost their lives through war and conflict. Then, bring your awareness to your breathing, and with each in-breath breathe in peace.

Deep Peace

> *Deep Peace of the running wave to you.*
> *Deep peace of the shining stars to you.*
> *Deep peace of the flowing air to you.*
> *Deep peace of the quiet earth to you.*

Advent

Advent brings us from the time of remembering the dead into the anticipation of a birth. The first Sunday after 30 November is the first Sunday of Advent. There are four Sundays in the lead-up to Christmas.

The word Advent, from Latin, means 'coming towards'. It invites us to think about what 'comes towards' us in this season. Just as we would await the birth of our own children, we can approach Christmas with awe, anticipation and making ready to receive the gift the Christ-child brings.

Traditionally Advent was a time for preparing and making everything ready, and this involved both inner and outer preparation. The house would be cleaned, everything washed and scrubbed and even the barn would be whitewashed. Within the Roman Catholic tradition everyone was expected to go to mass, even the 'hardy annuals' (who did not attend during the rest of the year) who made a special effort during Advent.

People were encouraged to give up meat and to fast on Fridays as a cleansing and preparation for the festivities ahead. This still makes sense today, given the richness of our Christmas feasting.

Wreaths of evergreens were made and laid on the table or suspended from the ceiling with four candles, one to be lit on each Sunday of Advent, until on Christmas Eve all four were lit. More recently there have been Advent Calendars, with glitter and pictures of stars and fruits revealed when the child opens her little windows, on the last day revealing the baby Jesus.

Advent is the time to write Christmas cards and letters to friends and family abroad. Many poorer Irish families eagerly awaited an 'American letter' from sons and daughters who had emigrated. This would contain news, greetings and a sum of money to help the family celebrate the season in style. It is also the time to make small gifts for those we love.

At Advent, country people went up to town with produce such as butter, eggs, chickens, geese and turkeys, to sell at the market. They exchanged presents with their town cousins and bought toys, gifts, new clothes and all the goods needed for the celebrations – candles, dried fruit, spices, sugar, sweets, tea, whiskey, wine and tobacco.

Nowadays we often feel overwhelmed by all we must do during this time – the preparations, cooking, shopping, writing cards and letters, carol-singing, Christmas fairs, concerts and fund-raising. Time feels shorter since daylight is scarce. We get exhausted and wonder where we can find the energy to cope with all these demands. It might help to remind ourselves that giving more sometimes helps us to do more than we thought we could – and we just might find that time expands too.

Festive food

The Christmas cake and pudding are usually prepared well in advance – usually in November, just after Hallowe'en.

Flour of Ireland, fruit of Spain
Met together in a shower of rain;
Put in a bag tied up with string,
If you tell me this riddle I'll give you a ring.

Christmas pudding

Ingredients:
4 oz / 110g raisins
8 oz / 225g currants
4 oz / 110g sultanas
4 oz / 110g candied peel
1 oz / 25g blanched almonds, chopped
4 oz / 110g plain flour
Pinch salt
1/2 tsp each ground ginger, nutmeg and
    mixed spice
8 oz / 225g dark brown sugar
4 oz / 110g brown breadcrumbs
8 oz / 225g butter cut into tiny pieces
Grated rind and juice of 1 lemon
2 beaten eggs
4 tbsp milk or porter (stout)

Method:
Mix all the dry ingredients in a large bowl.
    Rub in the butter. Add the fruit, nuts,
    peel, lemon rind and juice.
Stir in the beaten eggs and add enough milk
    or porter to make a soft mixture that will
    fall heavily from the spoon.
At this point you can stir in trinkets if you
    want to include these, e.g. a silver horse-
    shoe, ring, coin, wrapped in greaseproof

paper. Each member of the family should take a turn to stir the pudding and make a wish.

Grease two 1-pint pudding basins. Spoon mixture into the basins, leaving 2.5cm / 1 inch of space at the top for expansion.

Cover with greased greaseproof paper and a pudding cloth (a piece of muslin, a thin tea towel or aluminium foil will do) and tie this on with string.

Steam for 4 hours in a pot of water, topping up the water as necessary. You can store the puddings in a dry place until Christmas.

On Christmas Day you must steam the pudding for another 3 hours before serving.

Pour whiskey or *poitín* over the pudding and set it alight.

Serve with brandy butter, cream or custard.

Porter cake

Ingredients:
2 beaten eggs
1 lb / 450g plain flour
1 lb / 450g dried fruit
8 oz / 225g brown sugar
8 oz / 225g butter
2 oz / 50g glace cherries
2 oz / 50g mixed candied peel
4 oz / 110g almonds
Pinch nutmeg and mixed spice
$^{1}/_{2}$ pint / 275ml porter
Juice of 1 lemon

Method:
Preheat the oven to gas mark 4.
Line a deep 8-inch (20cm) cake tin with greaseproof paper.
Rub the butter into the flour.
Mix in all the dry ingredients.
Stir in the beaten eggs, lemon juice and porter.

Bake for $2^{1}/_{2}$ hours at gas mark 4 (180°C / 350°F). Allow the cake to cool in the baking tin, then store in an airtight tin.

Things to make and do

The Advent Garden

In Steiner schools a lovely Advent Garden tradition has developed. This gives children and adults alike a sense of mystery and anticipation.

A hall is cleared of all furniture. The windows are blacked out. Moss and greenery are brought in and arranged on the floor, leaving a long spiral path to a central candle. This path can be flat on the floor, or logs and stones can create a three-dimensional effect. The path is covered with pine needles to disguise the floorboards. Among the branches and moss there may be sparkling crystals and stones, flowers and wooden animals, shepherds and other figures.

A class, or classes, of children are led into the darkened room. All is in darkness save for the central candle, and perhaps a light over the 'angel' who plays the lyre or harp in a corner.

Another angel, usually an adult or someone from the oldest class, leads each child one by one to the start of the spiral path. The angel gives the first child an apple with a candle (see below for details). The child then walks the path at her own pace, lights her small candle from the flame at the centre and then places her little light somewhere within the garden.

The angel leads the next child to the path and gives him a candle apple, and so the process is repeated, each child placing his or her candle on or within the garden, until the room is filled with light.

'Nothing is said nor needs to be as the gentle incandescence of lyre strings sounds out the

simple magnificence of each child's journey in the presence of the whole school community.'
Alexander Mackenzie

The children are led out of the room to a feast of hot apple juice and biscuits.

Later, their apples are removed from the garden and they can then take one home with them.

Candle apples

You will need:
Rosy apples
Small candles

Method:
Polish the apples so that they are shiny.
Use a corer or knife to make a hole in the top of each apple, without going straight through.
Place the candle into the hole.

Advent wreath

You will need:
4 red candles
Florist's wire and thicker wire
Wire cutters
Scissors
Green twine
Red ribbon
Greenery – cypresses, fir branches, holly with
    berries, ivy, pine cones, etc

Method:
Tie greenery together in three bunches.
    Overlap the ends of one bunch with the
    beginning of the next and bind together
    with twine or florists' wire.
Bend to form a circle and tie with twine.
Wrap the twine around and around until the
    wreath is strong and has a good shape.
Cut sprigs of berry holly and place them
    amongst the greenery of the wreath. Fasten
    in place with florist's wire.
Add sprigs of ivy, pine and other greenery in
    the same way until the wreath is as full as
    you like.
Take one of the candles. Wind the thicker
    wire around the base of the candle several
    times and then use the wire to attach it to
    the wreath, concealing the wire among the
    greenery.
Repeat with the other three candles so that
    they are evenly spaced around the wreath.
Tie a bow of red ribbon and attach it with
    wire, or wrap red ribbon around the
    wreath and tie in a bow.
This wreath can sit in the centre of a table.

Hanging wreath

You will need:
Wreath made as above
Large curtain ring
Four long red ribbons
Stapler or needle and thread

Method:

Mark four equidistant points on the wreath.
Wrap ribbon around the wreath at each of
these four points and fasten off the
shorter ends with a needle and thread or a
stapler.

Gather the four long ends together into a
large curtain ring and sew or staple to
fasten them there.

This wreath can be suspended from a hook
in the ceiling.

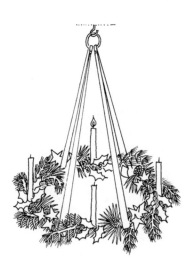

Walnut shell Advent calendar

You will need:
1 metre red ribbon or braid, 4cm /
   1½ inches wide
25 walnut shell halves
Gold paint
Small tokens – stones, stars, etc.
PVA glue
Small pieces of paper
Riddles, rhymes and mottoes
Gold thread

Method:

Ensure your walnut shells are neat
and then paint them gold. Write
rhymes or riddles on small pieces
of paper. Roll up tightly and
insert into a walnut shell.

Spread a layer of glue around the
rim of the walnut shell and stick
onto the ribbon about 10cm / 4
inches from the top.

Continue in this way, inserting
rhymes, stars, crystals, etc into
walnut shells and gluing them to
the ribbon. Leave approximately
1cm / ½ inch gap between the
walnut shells.

When all the shells are glued on,
trim the bottom of the ribbon as
shown.

At the top of the ribbon, fold over
the edge and sew neatly. Insert a
gold thread and tie this to make a
hanging string.

Hang the advent calendar on the
wall and remove one walnut each
day until Christmas.

On the next page are a few
suggestions for mottoes that you can
use in the advent calendar or in
Christmas crackers. If you can think
of any jokes include them too.

Tongue twisters

♣ She was a thistle sifter and sifted thistles through a thistle sieve.

♣ Red leather yellow leather, red leather yellow leather.

♣ A proper cup of coffee from a proper coffee pot.

♣ What noise annoys a noisy oyster? A noisy noise annoys a noisy oyster.

♣ A tutor who tooted the flute tried to tutor two tooters to toot.
   Said the two to the tutor: Is it harder to toot, or to tutor two tooters to toot?

Riddles (the answers are spelled backwards)

♣ Give it food and it will live. Give it water and it will die. What is it? (erif)

♣ What occurs once in a minute, twice in a moment but never in an hour? (m rettel eht)

♣ I run but I have no legs. What am I? (eson ruoy)

♣ Take me out and scratch my head. I've gone black where once was red.
   What am I? (hctam a)

♣ Remove the outside, cook the inside. Eat the outside, throw away the inside.
   What am I? (nroc)

Rhymes and sayings

♣ *Flour of Ireland, fruit of Spain*
  Met together in a shower of rain;
  Put in a bag tied up with string,
  If you tell me this riddle I'll give you a ring. (gniddup samtsirhc)

♣ *Christmas is coming, the geese are getting fat,*
  Please put a penny in the old man's hat.
  If you haven't got a penny, a halfpenny will do.
  If you haven't got a halfpenny, God bless you.

♣ *May you always have walls for the winds, a roof for the rain, tea beside the fire,*
  Laughter to cheer you, those you love near you, and all your heart might desire!

♣ *May the best day of your past be the worst day of your future.*
  May your pockets be heavy and your heart be light,
  May good luck pursue you each morning and night.

♣ *Dance as if no one were watching, sing as if no one were listening,*
  And live every day as if it were your last.

Christmas crackers

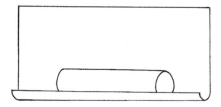

You will need:
Wrapping paper
4 toilet-roll tubes
Cracker snaps
Mottoes printed on small pieces of paper
 (see Advent calendar for suggestions)
Small gifts (crystals, etc) – optional
Ribbons
Paper glue
Scissors
Scraps of gold and silver paper

Method:
Cut paper to make a rectangle 16.5 x 38cm /
 6$^1/_2$ x 15 inches. Roll this around the
 toilet roll tube and glue it in place.

Insert the cracker snap into the tube along
 with the motto and gift.
Gather the paper together at the point where
 it reaches the end of the tube. Twist a
 little and tie a length of ribbon around it
 in a bow. Repeat for the other end of the
 cracker.
Cut shapes from gold or silver paper. Glue
 one on the outside of each cracker for
 decoration.

Celtic Christmas cards

Follow the instructions given in the All Souls
Day section to create a knotwork border for
the front of your card. Inside write an Irish
greeting.

Nollaig shona dhuit

or

Beannachtaí na Nollag

The crib

Many households have a stable and crib
scene with ox, ass, holy family, shepherds
and kings. Mary and Joseph can make their
way day by day towards the stable, gradually
getting closer as we approach Christmas.

Miniature pomander

You will need:
Kumquat
Cloves
Narrow ribbon (6mm)

Method:
Pierce the kumquat with the cloves, forming
a pattern of four lines of cloves running
from top to bottom.

Take the ribbon and wrap this around, as if
tying a parcel with string, so that it also
quarters the fruit. Tie in a knot and leave
about 7.5cm / 3 inches of ribbon, cutting
the ends of the ribbon on the slant.

These can be hung up in a wardrobe to scent
the clothes. They could also be used to
decorate the Christmas tree.

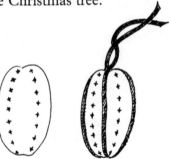

Carved pomander

You will need:
An orange, lemon or lime
Lino-cutting knife
Narrow ribbon to hang pomander – optional

Method:
Draw on the orange skin the pattern you
want to cut out. This can be as simple or
complex as you like. Regular beachball-
type stripes look very effective. Stars,
spirals and hearts also look good.

Use the lino-cutting knife to carve a pattern
into the orange skin. Be careful that you
always cut away from yourself, rather than
towards.

The fruit will gradually dry out, scenting the
room as it does. To hang, tie ribbon
around the pomander, leaving a loop.

Chocolate apricots

You will need:
Dried apricots
Bar of chocolate
Clear cellophane bags
Narrow ribbon

Method:
Melt the chocolate in a bowl over a pot of
simmering water.

Dip the apricots into the melted chocolate so
that they are half covered. Allow to dry
and harden.

Pack the chocolate fruits into clear
cellophane bags and tie with the ribbon.

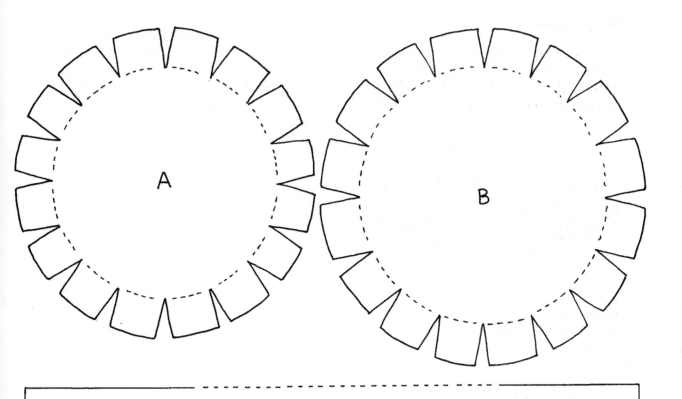

Length of side A = 21 cms
Length of side B = 23 cms

Round gift box

You will need:
Stiff card
Scissors
Glue
Clothes pegs
Tissue paper

Method:
Copy pattern A from the diagram onto your coloured card and cut out.

Fold up each of the little spikes and put a dab of glue on the outside of each. Attach the long strip of card to these, as shown.

Hold in place with the clothes pegs until the glue is dry.

Line the box with crumpled tissue paper.

For a lid, use pattern B, which is slightly bigger.

Sleep sachet

A lavender sachet placed under the pillow releases a relaxing scent and therefore aids a restful sleep. The sachet could also be placed in a drawer to scent clothes.

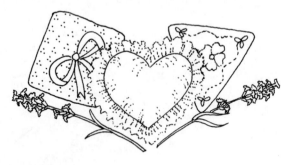

You will need:
Scraps of fine cotton fabric
Matching thread and needle
Lavender flowers
Scissors
Iron
Lace, ribbon or embroidery thread to
    decorate – optional

Method:
Copy a pattern from the diagram and cut out
    two pieces of fabric the same size and shape.
With the right sides of the fabric facing in,
    sew up the edges of the sachet with small
    stitches, leaving a gap at A-B.
Turn the right way out and iron flat.
Fill the sachet with lavender.
Sew up the remaining side neatly with small
    stitches. You can leave the sachet plain or
    decorate it with gathered lace, a ribbon tied
    in a bow or a little embroidered flower.

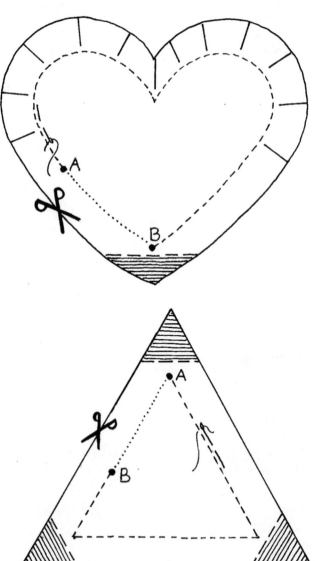

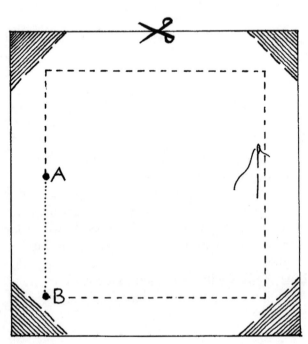

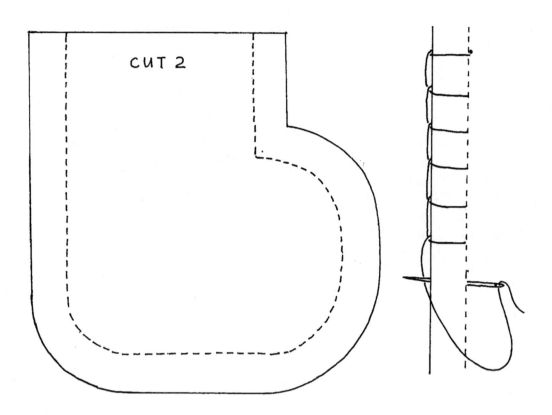

Little Christmas stockings

You will need:
Coloured felt
Thread and needle
Scissors
Thin ribbon, about 10cm / 4 inches

Method:
Copy the pattern from the diagram onto the felt and cut out two pieces.

Sew the two pieces together with a blanket stitch as shown.

Fold the ribbon to form a loop and sew this to the stocking.

You can put something small – like a stone, a sweet or some other little gift into the stocking and hang it on the Christmas tree.

Twelve days ring

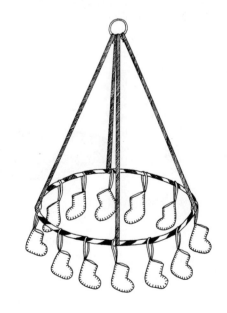

You will need:
Wire or willow hoop
12 little felt stockings
Small gifts
Ribbon to suspend the hoop

Method:
Make twelve of the little Christmas
stockings, as described above.
Suspend them from a wire hoop and hang
this from the ceiling with ribbons (see
Advent wreath for instruction).
Fill each stocking with a little gift, for
example a pencil sharpener, chocolate
coin, stone, for each of the twelve days of
Christmas.

Marzipan stuffed dates

You will need:
8 oz / 225g Marzipan
8 oz / 225g whole pitted dates
Paper doily

Method:
Soften the marzipan and roll it into sausages.
Cut dates open along one side and insert a
roll of marzipan. Close up the dates.
Place the dates on a paper doily in a round
gift box or in a clear cellophane bag and
tie with ribbon.

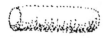

Gardener's hand cream

You will need:
4 parts sweet almond oil
4 parts coconut oil
3 parts white beeswax, grated
6 parts glycerine
Few drops lavender or geranium essential oil
Small jars with lids

Method:
Put the almond oil, grated beeswax and
coconut oil in a bowl over a pot of hot
water and allow them to dissolve slowly.
Stir. Add the glycerine a little at a time.
Remove from the heat and stir well until the
mixture is thick and creamy.
Add the essential oil and mix well.
Spoon into clean jars, cover with a cloth
until cool and then fasten on the lids.
Decorate the jar with your own label.

Winter solstice, 20-22 December

Thousands of years ago in Ireland massive stone structures, megalithic monuments, were built. Perhaps the best known of these are the mounds of Newgrange, Knowth and Dowth in the Boyne Valley in County Meath.

At Newgrange a grass-covered mound 80 metres in diameter and 13 metres high, faced with white quartz, sits within the remains of a stone circle. This is the largest tumulus in Ireland and with an estimated date of 3rd millennium BCE (Before the Christian Era), it is probably older than the Egyptian pyramids. It sits on a gentle rise in flat countryside and can be seen, on a clear day, from the hill of Tara. The base of the mound is faced with long stones laid on their sides and carved with complex spirals, lozenges, zigzags and diamonds.

Also known as Brugh na Boine, the mound of Newgrange is included in Irish legends as the home of Aoengus, one of the Tuatha de Danaan.

Before the entrance to the mound sits a massive stone, carved with the triple spiral symbol of trinity. The entrance portal leads to a long narrow passage, which draws one into a central chamber, from which three smaller chambers branch off in a cruciform shape. The walls of the inner chambers are decorated with carved symbols of sun and stars, and the cosmos is depicted as a living, moving, cyclical being.

Above the entrance there is another smaller opening which has a very special purpose. The entrance to Newgrange is aligned with the position of the sunrise on the shortest day of the year, winter solstice. For three days at the solstice the sun appears to stand still. If you were to observe the sunrise over a period of some weeks, you would see that its position moves along the horizon each day, except for the times of midsummer and midwinter solstices, when it rises from the same position for three days in a row.

Since the midsummer solstice, day length has been decreasing. At the autumn equinox, close to Michaelmas, day and night were of equal length. Since then the days have been growing shorter. At the midwinter solstice comes the shortest day. This is the darkest time of the year in the northern hemisphere. We experience this in our lives as hardship – it's cold and dark, we can feel alone and bereft. At this time of outer darkness, we can feel challenged to look within ourselves to find light.

Then at dawn on midwinter solstice, the first rays of the rising sun shine though the opening above the entrance to the mound of Newgrange, along the passage, and illuminate the carvings in the innermost chamber! One can imagine the awe of those ancient initiates who waited in darkness for this moment of the rebirth of the light. Many people nowadays spend years on a waiting list for the opportunity to witness the mystery of this solar event. One can understand why the birth of Christ, as lord of light, is celebrated at this time of year.

Things to do

Celebrate the solstice

We can mark this point in the wheel of the year's turning by rising early (but it's not too early at this time of year!) to greet the dawn. We might arrange with friends to meet at a special place – an ancient mound or dolmen, a stone circle or a high place – to watch the sunrise together. Remember to wrap up well and take a flask of hot apple juice and some cake to celebrate.

Newgrange sunrise at home

With a group of friends or family, you can recreate the Newgrange solstice sunrise.

You will need:
Thick curtains and blankets
Nightlights in jam jars – at least one for each participant
One large candle

How to do it:
Arrange the group sitting in a semi-circle around the large, unlit candle on the floor, facing East.
Lay the unlit nightlights in a row pointing towards the large candle.
Close all the curtains. In order to have complete darkness you may want to put blankets over any gaps where light is still shining through.

Set the scene by talking about the winter solstice and the need to look within to find our own inner light.
Tell the group about the Newgrange sunrise. Create an atmosphere of mystery.
Allow silence to descend and then light the first nightlight (i.e. the one furthest from the large candle).
Wait a few moments and then light the next, and so on. When all the nightlights are alight, light the large candle and let all bathe in the newborn sun.

CHRISTMAS

Christmas Eve, 24 December

On Christmas Eve family members make their way home to the parents' or grandparents' house for Christmas, bringing presents for all. This is the time for last minute cleaning and food preparation for the following day's dinner.

A search is made for the *bloc na Nollag,* a large log that is burned over the twelve days of Christmas.

As darkness falls, a candle is lit in the window to show travellers that they are welcome. One big candle, the *Coinneal mor na nollag,* is lit by the youngest person present and placed on the table.

The Christmas candle used to be placed in a holder made from a turnip, decorated with a little sprig of holly. The door was left unlocked and the table set with three places, a pitcher of milk and a loaf baked with caraway seeds and raisins in honour of the holy family on their journey.

Christmas Eve was traditionally a fast day. In older times people would eat nothing all day until the candles were lit at nightfall. Then they'd share a simple meal of white fish and potatoes, followed by a slice of Christmas cake, a glass of punch and storytelling round the fire. Children were told that on Christmas Eve an angel stands on each prickle of the holly leaf; that the gates of heaven are wide open and so anyone who dies at this time goes straight to heaven and that no sincere prayer on Christmas Eve goes unanswered. It is said that at midnight the animals kneel down in honour of the Christ child and that they have the gift of speech. However no one should try to spy on them.

The Christmas tree is still a fairly recent introduction to Ireland. In older times the home would be decorated with greenery, such as holly, ivy and mistletoe. Nowadays most households have a Christmas tree, bedecked with lights, and often have lights in trees

outside the house and around the roof eaves. Christmas Eve is a good time to install and decorate the tree, though it's probably best to have selected a tree and have it put aside well in advance!

Many people attend midnight mass in the churches, which are decorated with nativity scenes and echoing with rousing carols. Children watch the shining stars as they walk home from midnight mass, then hang up their stockings, pillowcases or sacks for Santy to fill with gifts.

*A*T LAST *Christmas Eve dawned. We brought in the holly which we had collected from the wood the previous Sunday and in a short time holly branches were growing from behind every picture – everywhere but around the clock, which was my father's sanctum and could not be touched. Then the Christmas tree. Our house was surrounded by trees: my father planted them all his life and he loved every one of them. At Christmas he suffered deciding which of his little ones had to be sacrificed. We usually ended up with a lop-sided branch instead of a full tree, but when it was dancing with Christmas cards and balloons it always seemed a beauty. We ran streamers across the kitchen and did everything our way while my mother made the stuffing and ignored the bedlam.*

A big turnip was cleaned and a hole bored in it for the candle; this was decorated with red-berried holly and placed in the window. That night no blinds would be drawn so that the light would shine out to light the way for Joseph and Mary. Before supper the Christmas log was brought in and placed behind the fire in the open hearth. Banked around with sods of turf it soon sent out a glow of warmth to make the toast that was part of our Christmas supper tradition. But before anything could be eaten the Christmas candle had to be lit. We all gathered round and my father lit the candle and

my mother sprinkled us with holy water. Then we sat around the kitchen table, my father at the top with my mother on his right and each of us in our own place. I feasted my eyes on the white iced cake, the seed loaf and barm brack, but most of all I gazed at the mountain of golden toast streaming with yellow butter. After supper we had lemonade and biscuits and the ecstasy of the gassy lemonade bubbling down my nose remains a memory that is Christmas for me.'

From *To School through the Fields*
by Alice Taylor

Things to make

Turnip candle holder

You will need:
Large red or white candle
Turnip or swede
Small sharp knife
Apple corer
Small plate
Holly and other greenery

Method:
Slice off the bottom of the turnip to make a flat base. Use an apple corer to make a hole in the turnip big enough to hold the candle. Using the small sharp knife, cut notches around the core hole to create a star pattern (see illustration).

Place the candle in the turnip, melting a little wax into the hole; while the wax is still soft, insert the candle and make sure that it is standing straight up. Decorate around the bottom of the turnip with holly and greenery.

Christmas Day, 25 December

Wish everyone 'Nollaig Shona Duit' –
Merry Christmas

Children wake early on Christmas day to see what gifts Santa Claus (known as Santy) has left in their stockings. After morning mass, the women of the house traditionally stayed home to prepare the Christmas dinner while the men went off to play hurling or other ball games together.

Some strict Presbyterians among the Ulster Scots did not celebrate Christmas at all, but continued with their everyday duties and responsibilities.

In coastal areas some hardy people go for a Christmas day swim, regardless of the weather! This is often used as a fundraiser for local charities.

The Christmas dinner is a rich feast and can last for many hours. The table is set with the finest cloth. The Christmas candle, amidst its greenery, sits at its centre. The best dishes are laid and a Christmas cracker is put at each place.

Festive food

The turkey is common as the Christmas bird these days, but the goose is still popular. The Limerick Ham and Spiced Beef were old favourites, served with a bread sauce, roast potatoes, parsnips, onions and Brussels sprouts.

Here are a few traditional recipes and a more contemporary vegetarian alternative.

Limerick ham

Ingredients:
1 smoked ham
Water to cover
2 tbsp brown sugar
Breadcrumbs
Whole cloves

Method:
Soak the ham overnight in water to dissolve the salt.
Next morning, pour away the water. Put the ham in a large pot and cover with water. Bring to the boil. Simmer on a low heat for 20 minutes per pound.
Remove from the pot and strip away any skin. Press a mixture of breadcrumbs and sugar onto the fat. Insert cloves.
Bake for 45 minutes in a moderate oven to glaze.

For the growing number of vegetarians, here is a lovely festive nut roast:

Cashew nut roast

Ingredients:
4 oz / 110g wholewheat breadcrumbs
8 oz / 225g cashew nuts
1 large onion
2 cloves garlic
1 tsp mixed herbs
Salt and pepper
2 eggs
A little milk or soya milk

Goose with apple sauce

You will need:
A goose
Sage, apple and onion stuffing
Apple sauce

Sage, apple and onion stuffing

Ingredients:
4 oz / 110g breadcrumbs
1 apple, 1 onion
1/2 oz / 13g chopped fresh sage
The white of 1 egg
Salt and pepper

Method:
Separate the egg. Beat the egg white. Mix all
the ingredients adding the egg last.
Stuff the goose and roast according to
weight, basting regularly, and pouring off
excess fat at the end.
While the goose is cooking, prepare the
apple sauce.

Apple sauce

Ingredients:
8 oz / 225g cooking apples
Small onion
1 oz / 25g sugar
1 tsp vinegar
1 oz / 25g breadcrumbs
Mustard, cinnamon

Method:
Peel, core and chop the apples. Peel and
chop the onion. Stew the apple and onion
in a pot together with the sugar.
When they are soft, add the breadcrumbs,
vinegar, mustard and cinnamon.
Add water or stock to make up for any liquid
lost. Simmer for 10 minutes.

For the filling:
4 oz / 110g grated cheese
Red or yellow pepper, sliced thinly
1 onion, chopped
Butter
1 egg

Method:
Preheat the oven to gas 5 (375°F/190°C).
Grind or chop the cashew nuts and put in a
  large bowl with the breadcrumbs.
Fry the chopped onion and crushed garlic in
  olive oil or butter until soft. Add to the
  nut mixture in the bowl.
Beat the eggs and milk with the salt, pepper
  and mixed herbs. Add the liquid to the
  nut mixture and stir well, adding more
  milk if it is too thick and heavy.
Leave to sit while you prepare the filling
  layer.

For the filling:
Cook the chopped onion and sliced pepper
  in butter or olive oil until soft but not
  browned.
Remove from the heat and add the grated
  cheese. The cheese will melt. Allow to
  cool a little and then add the beaten egg
  and stir again.
Line a loaf tin with greaseproof paper. Put in
  half of the nut mixture and level it off.
Add the filling and level that. Put the rest of
  the nut mixture over the filling and
  smooth the top.
Cover with a layer of greased greaseproof paper
  and bake in a warm oven for about 30-40
  minutes.

This course is followed by the Christmas
pudding – set alight on its serving platter
with whiskey or *poitín* (illegal home-distilled
alcoholic spirit made from potatoes) and
carried to the table in style.

Trifle is a Christmas treat, for those who find
the traditional pudding too heavy.

Sherry trifle

Ingredients:
1 lb / 450g trifle sponges
Custard
Tin of raspberries in syrup
5 fl oz / 130ml sherry
5 eggs
1 tbsp castor sugar
3/4 tsp real vanilla essence
1 1/4 pint / 845ml milk
1 pint whipped cream

Method:
Make an egg custard: Beat the eggs with the
  vanilla and sugar. Heat the milk to just
  below the boil and add to the eggs,
  beating all the time. Put into a heavy
  saucepan and stir over a gentle heat until
  thick enough. Do not let it boil!
Cut the sponges into 1cm / 1/2 inch slices and
  soak them in a bowl with the raspberries,
  syrup and sherry. Line the bottom of a
  large glass bowl with sponges.
Spoon in a layer of custard. Follow this with
  another layer of sponge. Spread the
  remaining custard over the top.
Cover and leave to sit for at least 4 hours,
  preferably overnight.
Spread whipped cream over the top of the
  trifle and decorate with glace fruit,
  crystallised flowers or grated chocolate.

After the Christmas dinner – which can take
a very long time – people sit around the fire,
telling stories, singing and playing games.

Carúl na Nollag

Andante

Focail: P Ní Uallacháin
Ceol : Traidisiunta

Dia do bheath'a Naí a - nocht A

rug - adh ins a' slab - la bocht go

ciúin gan caoi ad luas-cadh a luí Tá do

mháith-r-ín le do thaobh - sa

Carúl na Nollag (Christmas carol)   Music traditional, lyrics by Pádraigín Ní Uallacháin

Pronounced:

Dia do bheatha a Nai anocht   (gia do vaha nia noht)
A rugadh insa' stábla bocht   (ah ruga insa stabla boht)
Go ciúin gan chaoi ad' luascadh a luí   (go kooan gan cwee ad luscoo a lee)
Tá do mháithrín le do thaobhsa.   (tahdo wafreen ledda yoosha)

Anseo 'na luí sa mhainsérín   (ansho na lee sa wanshareen)
I gcró chúng an asailín   (a gro hoong an ashaleen)
Gean is grá ó Bheithilín   (gan as graw o behelleen)
Cuir síocháin I gcroí gach éinne.   (coor shiocane ee gree gach ainya)

Na haingle insna Flaithis thuas   (na hyngla insa flahish hoos)
Na haoirí a' triall ó shliabh anuas   (na heeri a treel o liu anose)
A' neosadh dúinn gur rugadh Críost   (a nyosu doin go rogo creeost)
'Tabhairt féirín uainn go léir dhuit.   (tor cherry noo inn go ler wit)

Dia do bheatha a Nai anocht   (gia do vaha nia noht)
A rugadh insa' stábla bocht   (ah ruga insa stabla both)
Go ciúin gan chaoi ad' luascadh a luí   (go kooan gan cwee ad luscoo a lee)
Tá do mháithrín le do thaobhsa.   (tahdo wa f reen ledda yoosha)

Carúl na Nollag

In English:

1

God be with you tonight little one
Born in the lowly stable
Quietly without tears rocking you to sleep
Your mother is by your side.

2

Here lying in the little manger
In the narrow shed of the little donkey
Love and affection from Bethlehem,
Bringing peace to the hearts of all.

3

The angels in the heavens above
The shepherds coming down the hill
Telling us that Christ is born
And bringing gifts for us all.

4

God be with you tonight little one
Born in the lowly stable
Quietly without tears rocking you to sleep
Your mother is by your side.

Wexford Carol

The Wexford Carol   An Irish carol from the 12th century

In English:

1

Good people all, this Christmas-time,
   Consider well and bear in mind
What our good God for us has done
   In sending his beloved Son.
   With Mary holy we should pray
To God with love this Christmas day;
   In Bethlehem upon that morn
There was a blessed Messiah born.

2

   The night before that happy tide
   The noble Virgin and her guide
Were long time seeking up and down
   To find a lodging in the town.
But mark how all things came to pass;
   From every door repelled alas!
   As long foretold, their refuge all
   Was but an humble ox's stall.

3

Near Bethlehem did shepherds keep
Their flocks of lambs and feeding sheep;
   To whom God's angels did appear,
Which put the shepherds in great fear.
   'Prepare and go', the angels said.
   'To Bethlehem, be not afraid,
For there you'll find this happy morn,
   A princely babe, sweet Jesus born.

4

With thankful heart and joyful mind,
The shepherds went the babe to find,
   And as God's angel had foretold,
They did our saviour Christ behold.
   Within a manger he was laid,
   And by his side the virgin maid,
   Attending on the Lord of life,
Who came on earth to end all strife.

5

There were three wise men from afar
   Directed by a glorious star,
And on they wandered night and day
   Until they came where Jesus lay,
And when they came unto that place
   Where our beloved Messiah was,
They humbly cast them at his feet,
With gifts of gold and incense sweet.

Some midwinter games

Consequences

Each player has a piece of paper and a pencil. The game leader, who can also play, calls out the order of things to be written (see below) and the players write on their paper, fold it over and pass it on to the next player, then all write the second item, fold again and pass it on; and so on. The list is:

1 girl's name
2 met ... boy's name
3 at ....
4 she did
5 he did
6 she said
7 he said
8 the consequence was ...
9 the world said ...

This forms a story – each paper has a different and crazy story.

Art consequences

This version works in the same way as consequences, but is suitable for children who cannot write. Each player draws a hat then folds the paper so that the next player sees just enough to draw the next part joining on to it and passes the paper on to her neighbour. Each player then draws a

face, folds the paper and passes it on, then an upper body, lower body, legs and feet.

Biographies

Each player has a paper and pencil and writes numbers 1 to 20. The player writes his name at the top of the sheet, and then is told to write the following:

1   a year after 1900
2   a place
3   a number less than 25
4   another place
5   yes or no
6   number less than 25
7   an occupation
8   a number, any size
9   another number
10 number under 50
11 a colour
12 another colour
13 part of the face
14 a bad habit
15 a sport or hobby
16 a flower
17 a kind of food
18 number under 1000
19 any number
20 a good or bad quality

When the papers are collected they are read as a biography, for example:

'*Ruth Marshall was born in (1) in (2). At the age of (3) she moved to (4), where she now lives. She is married or not (5) and has (6) children. She works as (7), earning (8) Euro a week and spending (9) Euro a week. Her shoes are size (10). Her hair is (11) and eyes are (12). Her most attractive feature is her (13). Her worst vice is (14), her hobby (15) Her favourite flower is (16), favourite food (17). She is expected to live to the age of (18) and her heirs will inherit (19) Euro. She will be remembered for her (20)*'

Confessions (no writing skills needed)

This game has three leaders, chosen in advance. One leader goes to each player in turn and whispers to her the name of another person whom she is supposed to 'be with'. The second leader whispers to each player a place or situation (e.g. up a tree, in the classroom, on horseback, asleep in bed, on a train to Belfast). The third leader whispers to each player a statement as to what the two are supposed to be doing (e.g. drinking champagne, cleaning the fridge, chopping firewood, feeding the pig....)

The three leaders do not know what each other have been saying. Then each player stands up and says what she has been told:

'I am Ruth Marshall and I am with Napoleon Bonaparte at Dublin Zoo, drinking champagne'
or
'I am Judith Evans and I am with Brian Boru at a jumble sale peeling potatoes'

Predicaments and remedies

Players sit in a circle. Each player writes on a slip of paper 'What would you do if ...' and finishes the question by naming a predicament of some kind.

On a second slip of paper the player also writes the remedy, or what he would do. He passes the predicament to his right and the remedy to his left, so that each player has two unrelated slips. Then one player reads out his predicament and remedy.

For example:

Predicament: *What would you do if your sandwiches fell in a puddle?*
Remedy: *Put on a sticking plaster.*

St Stephen's Day, 26 December

Throughout most of the year it was considered unlucky to harm a wren, except on St Stephen's day. It is said that the wren's chattering drew the attention of Roman soldiers to St Stephen as he lay hidden from them within a furze bush. This betrayal gave rise to the custom of hunting the wren.

Gangs of boys went on the wren hunt, chasing this tiny bird through the furze bushes. When they had caught and killed a wren they hung it in a holly branch tied to a pole bedecked with ribbons. Carrying this trophy they marched from house to house, singing and dancing, collecting money to help them 'bury the wren'. This was used to buy refreshments for a party later that day.

Known as the *Wren Boys,* the boys dressed in straw masks and costumes. In some places one dressed as a soldier with a sword, another as a fool and yet another as a female fool, while in parts of Kerry the Lair ban (the hobby horse) accompanied them.

Today, in many places the Wren Boys still go from door to door, singing and collecting money to help them 'bury the wren', but they no longer kill a wren.

Some say that the wren represents the spirit of the old year, which is slain by his son, the robin, representing the new.

The King of the Birds

*L*ONG LONG AGO *in a clearing in the great forest that covered the whole of the land, all the birds of Ireland came together to choose who should be their king. With pomp and ceremony the birds seated themselves in a circle, the great and the small together, preening themselves and settling their feathers and making ready for the decision-making that could last all day and into the next day.*

One by one around the circle each bird made his claim to the kingship.

'I should be King of the Birds because I am surely the most graceful of birds,' claimed Swan.

'Ah no, the honour should be mine,' claimed Heron, 'as I am surely the greatest of fishers.'

'I sing the sweetest of songs,' claimed Blackbird, 'so surely the crown is mine.'

'I have the most colourful plumage,' claimed Kingfisher, 'so I should make the most magnificent king.'

And so they continued as the day wore on. When it was eagle's turn to speak he said, 'Come now good friends. What is the one thing that sets us apart from all other creatures?'

'We eat worms!'
'We lay eggs!'
'We make nests!'
'We've got feathers!'

The birds called out all kinds of possible and impossible answers.

'No friends, it is the power of flight that sets us apart. I say that whichever of us can fly the highest should be King of the Birds.'

Owl spoke next. 'Well spoken, Eagle. Let us hold a contest to see who can fly highest.'

Eagle spoke again. 'Let you, Owl, as the wisest of birds, be the judge.'

Owl agreed, and flew to a high branch from which he could watch the contest. The other birds gathered together and at Owl's signal they rose as one. The air rang with the sound of flapping wings. The sky darkened as thousands of birds blotted out the sun.

Eagle, as could be expected, soon rose above the other birds who puffed and strained, their little hearts beating fast with the effort to reach higher and higher.

Owl, watching from his high branch, was about to declare Eagle the winner, when he saw a tiny bird one foot above him. It was Wren! Wren had concealed himself in the feathers of Eagle's back and now rose above him. By this time Eagle was wearied from his exertions and, try as he might, he could fly no higher.

When they had recovered themselves the birds gathered again in the clearing.

Owl crowned little Wren the King of the Birds, for he had flown even higher than Eagle.

The Wren Boys' Song

The wren, the wren, the King of the birds, on Stephen's day was
caught in the furze. Though he is little his family is great, so
rise up good people and give us a treat.

Gathering winter fuel

Good King Wenceslas looked out on the feast of Stephen
When the snow lay round about deep and crisp and even
Brightly shone the moon that night, though the frost was cruel
When a poor man came in sight gathering winter fuel.

If you happen to be gathering winter fuel,
here's a little rhyme that can help you to
learn what wood burns best:

Logs to burn

Oak logs will warm you well if they're old and dry.
Larch logs of pinewood smell but the sparks will fly.
Beech logs for Christmas time, yew logs heat well.
Scotch logs it is a crime for anyone to sell.
Beech logs will burn too fast, chestnut sears and all.
Hawthorn logs are good to last if cut in the fall.
Holly logs will burn like wax you should burn them green.
Elm logs like smouldering flax no flame is to be seen.
Pear logs, apple logs they will scent your room.
Cherry logs across the dogs smell like flowers in bloom.
But ash logs, all smooth and grey burn them green or old,
Buy up all that come your way, they're worth their weight in gold.

Anon

Mummers

There is a long tradition of Mummers' plays, dating back to early medieval times when craftsmen's guilds would each have performed their own play. They would perform throughout the twelve days of Christmas, moving from town to town. The main characters in these plays were the Hero, the Foreign Opponent, the Fool, the Giant, the Wise Man, the Doctor, and the He-She (a man dressed up as a woman). Usually the Hero is killed and is revived by the Doctor.

Perhaps the nearest we have to this today is the pantomime with its clearly defined heroes and villains, men in women's clothing and allusions to current political events. Most big towns in Ireland have a pantomime during the Christmas period.

Things to make and do

St Stephen's day was a fast day – probably a very good idea after the Christmas feast!

✦ Go visiting friends.

✦ Go for a long walk to work off some of the excesses of Christmas dinner.

✦ Go and see a pantomime or a mummer's play.

✦ Feed the birds.

Curoo, Curoo an 18th century carol

Full many a bird did wake and fly
Curoo, curoo, curoo
Full many a bird did wake and fly
To the manger bed with a wandering cry
On Christmas day in the morning
Curoo, curoo, curoo
Curoo, curoo, curoo

The lark, the dove, the red bird came
Curoo, curoo, curoo
The lark, the dove, the red bird came
And they did sing in sweet Jesus' name
On Christmas day in the morning
Curoo, curoo, curoo
Curoo, curoo, curoo

The owl was there with eyes so wide
Curoo, curoo, curoo
The owl was there with eyes so wide
And he did sit at sweet Mary's side
On Christmas day in the morning
Curoo, curoo, curoo
Curoo, curoo, curoo

The shepherds knelt upon the hay
Curoo, curoo, curoo
The shepherds knelt upon the hay
And angels sang the night away
On Christmas day in the morning
Curoo, curoo, curoo
Curoo, curoo, curoo

Winter bird cakes

Instead of hunting the wren, we can feed the little birds during the cold winter days!

Small birds can find food scarce in cold winters. You can help them by hanging these fatty food balls from trees in your garden. The fat binds the bird cakes together and provides instant energy for the birds.

You will need:
1 cup solid white vegetable fat
3 cups mixed grains and seeds (e.g. whole oats, chopped nuts, flaked maize, kibbled wheat, millet, sunflower seeds, chopped raisins. You can vary the quantities according to what you have available)
or 3 cups of ready mixed wild bird seed
Wire or plastic mesh

Method:
Slowly melt the fat in a large pan over a gentle heat.
Add the grains, seeds and nuts and stir well until the fat is really well mixed in.
Dampen your hands, take handfuls of the mixture and form into small balls or cakes. As the mixture cools the fat will solidify and hold the grains and seeds together.
Wrap the fat balls in wire or plastic mesh and hang them from a tree or a bird table.

Pine cone bird feeder

You can also make a bird feeder from a large pinecone. To do this:

Tie a length of string to a large open pinecone.
Make up the food mixture as before and, while it is still warm, spread it over the pinecone.
Tie the pinecone to a tree or bird table.

New Year's Eve, 31 December

This was a notable festival in Ireland only in areas where Scottish influence was strong, like parts of Ulster. In Scotland, with the influence of Presbyterianism and Calvinism, Christmas was celebrated with little festivity or joy, but New Year, as a secular festival, gave an opportunity to let one's hair down!

1 January has been the New Year only since 1751 when the new calendar was established. New Year traditions in Ireland are therefore largely the well-known Scottish customs of first-footing, ringing of bells at midnight, fireworks and divination.

First-footing

Good luck for the coming year depended upon the appearance of the first person to enter the house after midnight. The best first-footer is a tall black-haired man. If there isn't a dark man, then a dark boy will do, or even a black cat, but the worst possible luck is associated with a red-haired woman – so don't let her in until someone else has stepped over the threshold!

Divination

Divination rites like those at Samhain/Hallowe'en were practised on New Year's Eve. If a girl put a sprig of holly and ivy or mistletoe under her pillow and said the following verse, she might have dream of her future husband.

Ivy green and holly red,
Tell me whom I shall wed.

Oíche na Coda Móire

(Night of the big portion). Eating a large meal on New Year's Eve ensures that there is plenty of food in the house throughout the coming year.

Breaking bread to keep hunger at bay

Bake a large *barm breac* (fruit loaf). Make sure that all the doors and windows of the house are closed. The woman of the house takes up the cake and knocks it on each door and window while saying the following three times:

We warn Famine to retire beyond these shores from this night to this night twelvemonth and even this very night.

In other places the man of the house takes up the bread and throws it against the main door. Everyone present takes up a bit of the broken bread to eat.

Looking back and looking forward

New Year's Eve is a good time to take stock of our lives. We might sit quietly alone or in a group and review the events of the past year – both personally and globally. This gives us a chance to think about how we have behaved, what we have achieved, what we'd like to have done differently, what joys and sorrows we have encountered in the last twelve months.

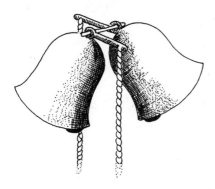

At midnight you can write on a piece of paper what you would like to clear out of your life. Then write on another piece something that you would welcome into your life. Take the two slips of paper to the open fire and cast them into the flames, with gratitude for the lessons you've learned from the past year.

New Year's resolutions

This is the time for making New Year's resolutions. Ask yourself what do you intend to do this year? Is this real, do you really mean it? Can you stick to it, and work at this right through the year?

This year I intend to share my toys with my little sister.

This year I intend to do my homework as soon as I get home from school.

This year I intend to keep my bedroom tidy.

This year I intend to be patient and understanding with my children, especially when they are making a racket.

This year I intend to learn how to play the saxophone ... cook nourishing wholefood meals for my family ... use the car less and the bicycle more ... visualise world peace ... meditate regularly ... go for a jog each morning ...

Write the following on a piece of decorated paper.

This year I intend to: ...

Now post your resolution somewhere that you can see it and remind yourself of your intention for the year.

Nollaig na mBan, 6 January

Also known as Women's Christmas, Little Christmas, Epiphany, Three Kings' Day

Epiphany is known in Ireland as Little Christmas or Nollaig na mBan, meaning the women's Christmas. It was celebrated with a lighter feast than the Christmas dinner. The feast includes sandwiches, little cakes and dainties.

The Three Wise Kings have now arrived bearing their gifts of gold, frankincense and myrrh to the infant Christ.

It is said that on Three Kings' Night water turns to wine. However, it is not a good idea to try and take advantage of this for anyone who does will suffer some dreadful fate. A story tells that three stones near St Brendan's Well in Ventry, County Kerry, are the petrified remains of three men who attempted to spy on the miracle and drink their fill of wine.

On 7 January the Christmas tree is taken down, and decorations packed away until next year. The greenery is taken down and saved for the cooking fire on Shrove Tuesday to warm the pancake pan. The stable/crib however remains in place, with the three kings there now, until St Brigit's Day.

Festive food

Dainty sandwiches

On this special occasion you can remove the crusts and cut the sandwiches into triangles.

Ingredients:
Thinly sliced bread – wholemeal or white
Vegetable margarine or butter

Sandwich fillings:
Cream cheese
Finely grated carrot
Alfalfa sprouts
Cucumber

Method:
Spread butter or margarine on the thinly sliced bread. Cut off the crusts.
Spread a layer of cream cheese or houmous. Add thinly sliced cucumber, grated carrot and alfalfa sprouts.
Top with another slice of bread. Cut the sandwich into triangles and display on a doily on a fancy plate.

Rice cake open sandwiches

Ingredients:
Packet rice cakes
Cottage cheese
Sliced cucumber
Shredded red and yellow peppers
Sliced kiwi fruit
Parsley to garnish

Method:
Spread cottage cheese on the rice cakes.
Arrange cucumber slices, peppers or kiwi fruit slices artistically on top.
Garnish with a little sprig of parsley.

butterfly buns

Queen cakes

Ingredients:
5 oz / 135g flour – white or wholemeal
1 tsp baking powder
4 oz / 110g castor sugar
Grated rind of $^1/_2$ lemon or orange
2 beaten free-range eggs
4 oz / 110g vegetable margarine
1 tbsp water

Method:
Preheat the oven to gas mark 6 (200°C / 400°F). Line a bun or cupcake tray with paper cases.
Cream the margarine and sugar in a bowl. Add the beaten egg and beat well.
Sift the flour into the bowl and fold it into the mixture, adding a little water if necessary to make a dropping consistency.
Spoon into the paper cases. Bake for 15 to 20 minutes.

Butterfly buns

Ingredients:
As queen cakes, plus
Whipped cream
Raspberry jam

Method:
Follow the recipe for queen cakes.
When the buns are cool, slice off the top of each bun and cut these in half. These small pieces will become the butterfly wings.

Spread raspberry jam on the bottom part of each bun and add a blob of thick cream.
Replace the two cut off pieces, arranging them like wings on the cream. Dust the tops with icing sugar.
Arrange the buns on a paper doily on a pretty plate.

Things to make

The Three Kings arrive at the manger with their gifts. Melchior, dressed in red, brings his gift of gold. Balthazar, in blue, brings incense, while Caspar, in green, brings myrrh.

Gold gift box

(see next page)

You will need:
Gold card
Scissors or craft knife
Glue

Method:
Copy the template from the diagram onto the gold card and cut out a base and a lid for your box.
Glue together as shown.
Fill the box with a small gift and give to a friend today.

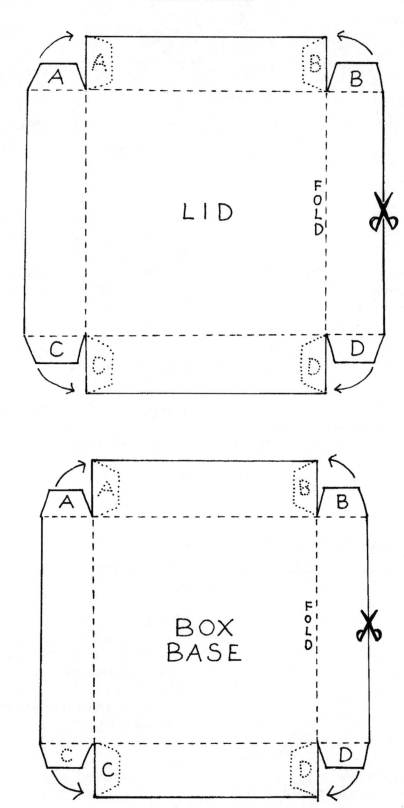

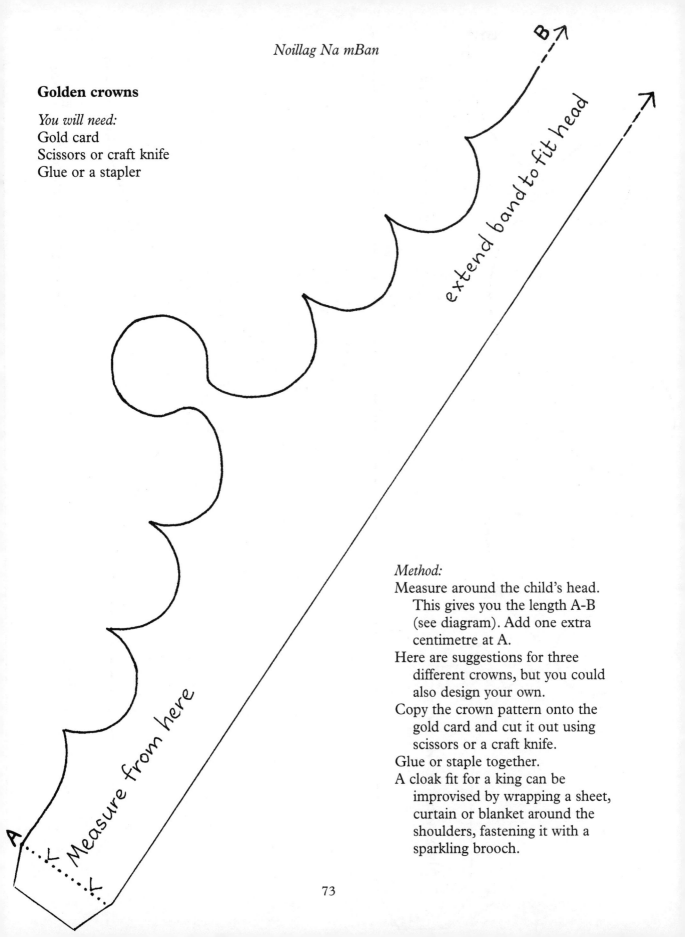

Golden crowns

You will need:
Gold card
Scissors or craft knife
Glue or a stapler

B↗

extend band to fit head

↗

Measure from here

A
✂
✂

Method:
Measure around the child's head. This gives you the length A-B (see diagram). Add one extra centimetre at A.

Here are suggestions for three different crowns, but you could also design your own.

Copy the crown pattern onto the gold card and cut it out using scissors or a craft knife.

Glue or staple together.

A cloak fit for a king can be improvised by wrapping a sheet, curtain or blanket around the shoulders, fastening it with a sparkling brooch.

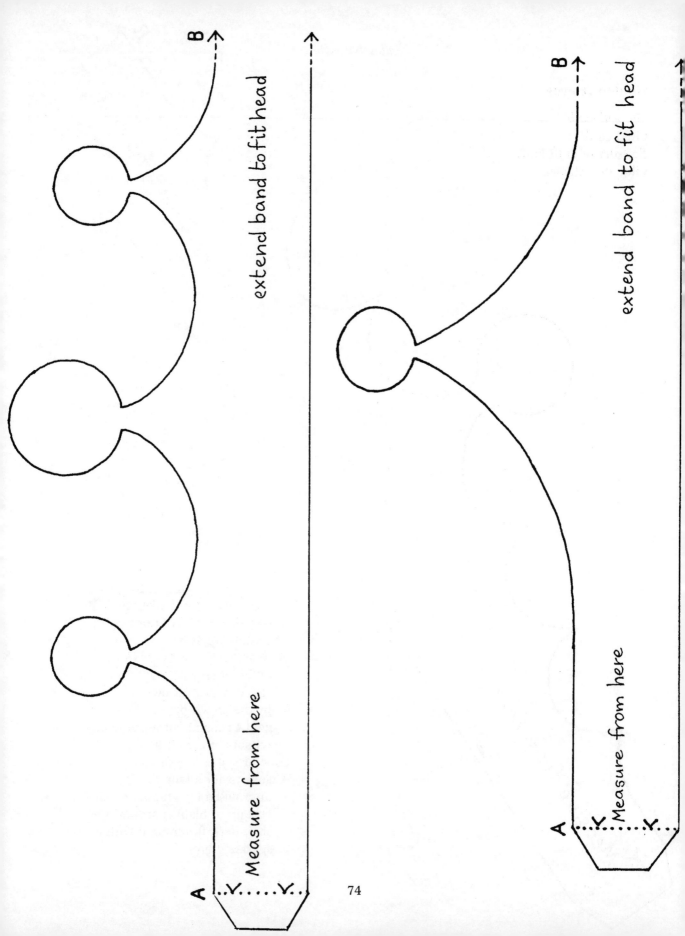

extend band to fit head

Measure from here

A

B

extend band to fit head

Measure from here

A

B

74

Winter to Spring

Imbolc

Imbolc, 31 January – 1 February

Also known as St Brigit's Day, Lá Fheile Bríde

1 February is known as the first day of spring. This may seem a little unusual, as there are few outward signs of what we usually think of as spring. Few flowers are as yet peeping through the hard earth, save for the snowdrop and, a little later, the humble dandelion – both sacred to St Brigit – and brighter weather still seems far off.

However, within the context of the agricultural year, Imbolc marks the loosening of winter's grip. The time from Samhain to Imbolc was known as a time of little sun. Now the days are becoming visibly longer, even if the weather remains cold and wet! It used to be said that from St Brigit's day you could 'put away the candlestick and half the candle'.

The word 'Imbolc' is thought to be derived from an old Gaelic word meaning 'ewe's milk'. At this time of year, the sheep's milk begins to flow in preparation for lambing.

Brigit, as the bright maiden of spring, bringing light and the possibility of new growth, takes over from the Cailleach, the hag of the dark winter time. The fertility of the land is reawakened and preparations for spring sowing begin.

Brigit is a fascinating character, beloved of the Irish. She is one face of the original mother goddess, the sun, the earth and all creation. She is later found amongst the Celtic pantheon as one of the Tutha De Danann. Daughter of the Dagda (the 'good god'), she is a trinity in herself, seen as the source of fertility, abundance, of all life within nature, and was known as a master or goddess of the elements. She is the beloved patron of poets, and her two sisters, also named Brigit, are patrons of healing and smithcraft. A fire goddess, she feeds the fires of inspiration, of the life spark, and the physical fire that transforms metals. A sacred flame was kept alight in her honour.

With the advent of Christianity, Brigit the saint acquired many of the attributes of the goddess. Brigit has served as a bridge, allowing continuity between the old and new. Many of the stories of the saint are drawn from memories of the nourishing, generous goddess.

It is said that the Irish took to the Christian faith so easily because they recognised its trinity as the sacred trio with which they had long been familiar. Mary, the mother of Christ, they saw as a personification of Brigit, who was known as 'Mary of the Gael'. Legends tell that Brigit was the daughter of the innkeeper who gave the holy family shelter in his stable. Brigit is said to have nourished the baby Jesus at her own breast. By acting the fool, she distracted the guards who searched on King Herod's orders during the slaughter of the innocents, and helped Mary to escape with her babe unharmed.

Brigit's Childhood

*S*T *BRIGIT was the daughter of Dubthach, a nobleman and Broisceach a cowherd slave. Whilst out in the chariot together, a druid spying the pair said that their daughter would shine like 'a radiant sun among the stars of heaven'. Dubthach sold Broisceach to a druid. Brigit was born at sunrise as her mother stepped over the threshold, a vessel of milk in her hand, with one foot within and one without the house.*

The druid raised her as his own daughter. When her mother tried to wean her, the infant Brigit could keep down no food until a miraculous white, red-eared cow arrived to provide milk for her. One day the druid saw three angels baptising the child, and they spoke to him and told him that she should be named Brigit, which means 'fiery arrow'.

One day her mother went to tend the cattle in the fields, leaving Brigit asleep in her cot. She heard cries that a great fire had broken out and ran back to see her home apparently ablaze amidst a pillar of fire. When one brave man burst into the flames, he found that the source of the fire was Brigit herself, still peacefully asleep and unharmed.

This same fire was to appear around Brigit on a number of occasions. Once she had established a centre at Kildare *(Kil* – church or cell, *dara* – oak, the tree of the druids) a fire was kept alight by 19 women who took it in turns daily to tend the flame. On the 20th day, Brigit herself would tend the fire. Oak trees were sacred to the druids, so the choice of this spot to build a community suggests continuity with older beliefs. This fire was kept alight until the time of the dissolution of the monasteries in the 15th Century.

Now, however, there is a growing revival of interest in Brigit goddess and saint, who personifies the generous nourishing feminine face of Celtic spirituality. A 'Feile Bride' is held each year at Kildare and the sacred flame has been rekindled.

In recent years a light from Kildare was taken to Beijing for the global conference for the advancement of women.

As with the other quarter days, the festivities begin on the eve of the feast day. On 31 January the girls and women would make a Brideóg, a kind of doll or model of Brigit, by wrapping a bundle of straw or reeds in a white dress and shawl. The party would then carry the Brideóg in a procession from house to house offering Brigit's blessing to those who invited them in. This would finish with a feast on the proceeds. Sometimes the Brideóg was made from the last sheaf of the previous harvest, the Cailleach.

Brigit's cross

One of the family members, sometimes the man, other times the eldest girl, would go out and gather a bundle of rushes to make Brigit's crosses. The rushes were to be pulled rather than cut.

On his return he would lay the rushes on the doorstep and knock on the door. He would then walk clockwise around the house and come again to the door and knock. Once more he walks around the house and knocks at the door.

Once he has completed his third circuit of the house he calls, 'Get down on your knees, open your eyes and let Brigit in'.

The others reply, 'She is welcome, she is welcome, she is welcome.' The rushes are laid under the table and a feast is held of colcannon, dumplings, boxty, fresh churned butter.

After the meal, or the next day, the Brigit's crosses were made, blessed and hung above the door of the dwelling house and the byre. Children hung their own smaller crosses over their beds.

The Brigit's cross offered protection from fire, lightning, infectious diseases and the evil eye.

There are four main styles of Brigit's cross, each popular in different parts of Ireland, but now the best known is the 'swastika' cross, which was used for many years by Radio Telefis Eireann as its emblem.

The crois

The crois is Brigit's girdle or belt. Communities in the west of Ireland made a giant girdle out of twisted straw rope. Three lengths of straw rope were twined and then plaited together. The two ends were bound to make a continuous loop. Three small crosses of straw were attached to the belt. The belt was then taken from house to house. To pass through Brigit's girdle was to receive a threefold blessing. The custom was that one walks three times through the crois, walking in a figure of eight pattern.

Brigit's cloak or Brat Bríde

Brigit's cloak was known for its miraculous powers. When St Brigit asked the king of Leinster to grant her land to establish her community, he said she could have as much land as her cloak could cover. Brigit removed her cloak and as she laid it on the earth, it unrolled and spread until it covered a large part of the area known as the Curragh of Kildare!

Brigit's cloak is known for the protection it provides to the people of Ireland. On the eve of St Brigit's Day, it was customary to lay a piece of cloth as Brigit's cloak on a bush or a rooftop overnight. St Brigit was said to walk throughout the country on that night with her beloved white cow and whatever she touched she would bless. The cloak or item of clothing would then offer the wearer protection. Fishermen might leave out their jumpers as a protection against drowning. Sore throats, headaches, sickly animals or lambs rejected by their mothers would be wrapped in the Brat Bridhe. The fairies could not take a baby who was wrapped in Brigit's cloak.

Sometimes a ribbon, known as Ribin Bríde, was tied to the door latch overnight and then tied around the head as a remedy for headache. St Brigit herself was said to suffer from headaches.

Often people would leave out a bowl of water, milk, butter or salt for Brigit to bless as she passed through the land. They would also leave a bundle of oats for her cow. The blessed food might be shared or given to the needy or kept for its curative properties.

A few seed potatoes or corn seeds left out on St Brigit's Eve would be mixed in with all the seed for the spring sowing.

Festive food

Fresh butter would be churned on St Brigit's Eve, the milk being saved for days beforehand for this occasion. The new milk was welcome and would form a major part of the feast. The festive table would be filled with sowens (a milky porridge), colcannon, boxty, dumplings and *barm breac*. As most of these have been covered elsewhere (see Samhain for colcannon, boxty and *barm breac)*, here are some new ideas for festive foods for Imbolc.

Decorate the festival table with a white cloth or shades of green, yellow or cream. A pot of snowdrops in bloom, or a dandelion, as Brigit's flowers, would be appropriate, and a white or green candle and a Brigit's cross.

Bread Bogha Bríde

Method:

Make up a yeast bread dough. Grease a large flat baking tray. Divide the dough into one large and three smaller pieces.

Take the three small pieces and roll out to form long strands on a well-floured surface. Plait these to form a long plait. Cut in half and lay one over the other to form a cross. Place in the centre of the baking tray.

Take the other piece of dough and divide it into three. Roll out and plait as before.

Form this plait into a circle around the cross. Bake at gas 4 or 5 (350°F / 180°C) for 20 minutes or until done.

Milk and honey scones

Brigit was not only a cowherd, but also a beekeeper. These simple scones combine these two symbols of Brigit.

Ingredients:
8 oz / 225g wholemeal flour
4 tsp baking powder
2 oz / 50g butter or margarine
2 tbsp clear honey
8 tbsp milk

Method:

Set oven to gas mark 8 (450°F / 230°C). Sift flour and baking powder into a bowl. Rub in the butter.

Add the milk and honey and mix to form a soft dough. Roll out on a floured surface to about 2.5cm / 1 inch thick. Cut into rounds and place on a floured baking sheet.

Bake for 12-15 minutes. Cool and eat with fresh butter, jam or curd cheese.

Butter

You will need:
Cream
Glass jar with a screw top

Method:

Wash and thoroughly dry the jar and lid.

Pour the cream into the jar. Tighten the lid and shake continuously. The cream will thicken, becoming whipped cream.

Keep shaking until it forms yellowish lumps and separates out. Pour off the liquid and gather the lumps of butter together.

Yoghurt

You will need:
Milk – skimmed or whole milk according
   to taste
Vacuum flask
Tub of natural live yoghurt or yoghurt starter

Method:
Make sure the flask is completely clean.
Heat the milk to just below boiling point,
   then remove from the heat. Allow it to
   cool to body temperature.
Mix the live yoghurt into the warm milk and
   pour into the flask. Seal and leave to sit
   until cool.
Pour into a bowl and keep in the fridge until
   needed.

You can use your own yoghurt to start
another batch, though after a few weeks, it
may be best to start again with a commercial
culture.

Curd cheese

Ingredients:
1 pint / 570 ml milk
Lemon juice

Method:
Warm the milk and allow to cool to body
   temperature. Stir in the lemon juice. The
   milk will begin to curdle. Let it sit for a
   while and then pour into a muslin cloth in
   a strainer.
Gather the four corners of the muslin
   together and suspend over a bowl while
   the whey slowly drips out. When it has
   finished dripping, open the muslin, remove
   the curds and put in a bowl.
You can flavour your soft cheese with herbs
   or spices. Chopped chives, parsley, garlic
   or paprika are all tasty additions to curd
   cheese.

Ginger beer

St Brigit was famous for her hospitality. She
brewed beer and always had enough to meet
the needs of her guests. One Easter there was
a large gathering and the beer was running
out. Brigit took the last existing barrel and
blessed it, and it provided good cheer for all
the guests.

This recipe makes a fizzy non-alcoholic
ginger beer. To have it ready for St Brigit's
Day start the process a few days in advance.

Ingredients:
1 handful of fresh ginger root
1 lb / 450g cups of sugar
8 pints / 5 litres water
1/2 tbsp bread yeast
2 lemons
1/4 tbsp cream of tartar

Method:
Grate or finely slice the root ginger and the
   lemon peel and squeeze the juice from the
   lemons. Put in a large bowl with the sugar
   and cream of tartar.
Pour the boiling water into the bowl and stir
   until the sugar dissolves. Leave to cool
   until hand hot.
Meanwhile sprinkle the dried yeast and a
   teaspoon of sugar into half a cup of
   lukewarm water. Leave for 10 – 15
   minutes in a warm place and then stir.
Add the yeast to the bowl and stir it in. Cover
   the bowl with a cloth and leave in a warm
   place to ferment for 24 hours. Being
   careful not to disturb the sediment, strain
   the liquid through muslin and then pour
   into bottles.
Fasten the bottles securely and leave them in
   a cool place for two or three days.

Things to make

St Brigit's crosses

Sunwheel or swastika type

This is the best known of the St Brigit's crosses, although not the most common in older times.

You will need:
Scissors
Bundle of rushes *(Juncus effusus* or *Juncus conglomerates.* These are common and grow abundantly in damp and boggy places)
String or wool

Method:
Take two long straight rushes (A and B).
Fold one rush in half (B) and place it over the straight rush (A) at right angles.

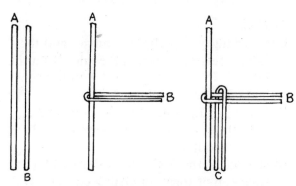

Fold another rush (C) and loop it over B.
Turn through 90 degrees to the left then fold another rush (D) and loop it over C.

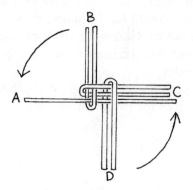

Turn through 90 degrees and continue in this way until the cross is the required size.

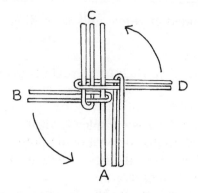

Tie off each leg of the cross tightly with coloured yarn. Trim the rushes neatly to finish.

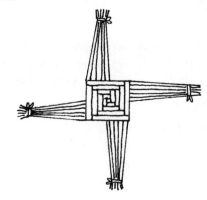

Diamond cross

This was the most common type of St Brigit's Cross, originally made of straw or lake rushes. If you use coloured yarn you can create stripes of different colours.

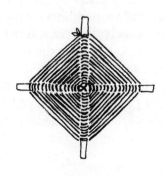

You will need:
2 sticks or kebab skewers
Wool or string

Method:
Lay the two sticks to form a cross and tie together with yarn.

Begin to bind by bringing the yarn over stick A, round behind A and over A once more.

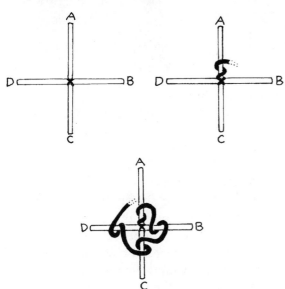

Bring the yarn over B, around it and over again. Bring yarn over C, behind and over C once more.

Continue in this way, winding the yarn clockwise around the cross until the diamond is the desired size. Fasten off the yarn.

Once you have mastered this basic diamond cross, you can go on to make a more complex cross by adding smaller diamonds at the ends of the sticks, as shown.

Interlace cross

You will need:
18 or 24 rushes
Scissors
Yarn to bind

Method:
Divide your rushes into six bundles, each containing 3 or 4 rushes.

Lay three bundles in rows on a flat surface, with the same distance between them.

Weave the other three bundles through these at right angles.

Arrange so that the weaving is regular

Gather each set of three ends together, being careful to create a gentle curve and bind tightly with yarn.

Trim off the excess rushes neatly.

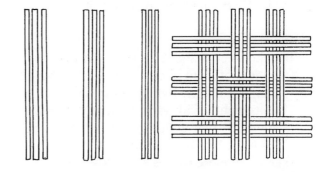

Brideóg

You will need:
Bundle of rushes or straw
String or wool
Scissors
Scraps of white and green cotton fabric for her dress and cloak
About 15cm / 6 inches of white ribbon

Method:
Take between 8 and 12 rushes and make a bundle of them about 45cm / 18 inches in length. Find the halfway point and tie there tightly with yarn. Fold at the tie. Tie another string tightly about 1 inch down from the fold to form the head.

Take three more rushes and place these through the body, just below the head to form arms. Tie tightly below the arms.

Fold the arms round and fasten them together with yarn. Trim off the excess rushes from the arms and base.

To dress the Brideóg:
Cut a rectangle of white fabric long enough for a skirt and wide enough to gather around the Brideóg.

Hold the skirt in place and tie a string around the waist.

Wrap the ribbon as shown, beginning behind the waist, coming to the front, crossing over the chest, around behind the neck, and crossing over the chest again; and once more around the waist to cover the string holding the skirt on. Wind a coloured thread around this several times and tie off to hold in place.

To make the cloak, take a rectangle of green fabric and a lay a short piece of yarn about an inch or two from the top of it. Fold the fabric over the yarn. Tie the yarn around the doll's neck as a cloak.

Gabhaim Molta Bríde

Gabh - aim mol - ta Brí - de

Ion - mhain í le hÉir - inn

Ion - mhain le gach tír - í

Mol - aim - is go léir í

Gabhaim Molta Bríde

	Pronounced:
Gabhaim molta Bríde	(gowan molta breeda)
Ionmhain i le hEirinn	(on wan ee la herrin)
Ionmhain le gach tir I	(on wan leg ach teeree)
Molaimis go leir i.	(molamish go leri)
Lochrann geal na Laighneach	(lochran gal na line ach)
A soilsiu feadh na tire,	(a solshoo fah na teera)
Ceann ar oghaibh Eirean,	(kyan ar ogiv errin)
Ceann na mban ar mine.	(kyan na man ar meena)
Tig an geimreadh dian dubh,	(teegan gerra deean duv)
A' gearradh lena gheire,	(a garru lenna gerra)
Ach ar la 'le Bríde,	(ach ar lawla breeda)
Gar duinn Earrach Eireann.	(gardoon arrach errin)

Translated:

All praises to Brigit, beloved of all Ireland. Beloved of all lands is she, let us now all praise her.

Bright torch of Leinster, shining through the whole land, finest of Ireland's maidens, most gentle of all women.

Winter has been hard and dark, has cut us with its keenness, but on the day of Brigit's feast, Ireland's spring is near.

The Green Lady

A FEW years ago now, on St Brigit's Day, I was up in Galway city. The town was busy, the Saturday market packed with people buying olives, sun-dried tomatoes, sourdough bread, ethnic clothes from Thailand and Nepal, houmous and cheese amidst the local crafts, vegetables and eggs. I didn't have much money in those days, being a single mother of a young child, and whenever I'd visit the city I'd do the rounds of the charity shops looking for bargains.

In those days I practised a form of Raja Yoga and I had come up to the city that weekend for a meditation gathering where people could sit together with a teacher of this discipline. I arrived too early for the gathering and the hall was still locked. I had a little money with me – enough to pay the conference fee and my whole week's food and fuel, so I set off to the shops.

I wore a brown leather backpack, with my waterproof jacket and my packed lunch inside and my purse in a pocket on the outside.

I walked along the riverside; the water was high and the bright wintry sun sparkled on its surface as it flowed by. I made for the charity shops first. Walking up Quay Street, I noticed a tall woman, dressed in green. She stood out from the crowd somehow, maybe because she had on an interesting hat, or because she was so tall. I wandered from shop to shop, looking at things I couldn't afford and thinking, 'Would my life really be better if I had that?' Difficult as things were at times, I didn't think these material goods could feed my soul. Meanwhile all around me people were buying, spending, as a way of life. Walking out of a bookshop I saw her again. In my mind I started to call her 'The Green Lady'. Now, when I say she was dressed in green, I mean totally dressed in green – hat, shoes, jacket, skirt, gloves, everything! Everywhere I went I caught sight of her moving through the crowds.

I looked at my watch – there was only half an hour to go now. I walked towards a narrow alley that I knew would lead me to the riverside street with the gathering hall. Ahead of me I saw her again, the Green Lady, turning into the alleyway. Like most cities these days, Galway has its share of beggars on the streets. Two young people sat on the pavement huddled against the cold beside their bags. An old scarf spread out before them held a few coins. I saw, ahead of me, the Green Lady bend down and give the young couple a tray with two cups of tea, two burger rolls and salad. She walked on, fading into the crowd.

I thought, 'Is that not really sweet? How much more appropriate than giving money!' When I reached the young couple I stopped to say that I hoped they would enjoy their meal. The young man beamed a beautiful smile at me. Somehow I felt blessed. I walked on, thinking to myself, 'How can I not find it in my heart to give what is needed, when it is needed? Why is my heart so closed?' I walked on, savouring the sweetness of the Green Lady's simple gift, as if she had given something precious, not just to the couple, but also to me. I looked to see where she had gone. I wanted to speak to her, tell how touched I was, but she was nowhere to be seen.

I reached the hall and the doors were open now. At the registration desk, I took off my bag to bring out my purse, and discovered the zip pocket was open, and my purse gone! As I stood shocked, the woman behind the desk recognised my genuine distress and told me to go in without paying. I found a seat, out of the way, and let the shock of violation sweep over me. How could I put food on the table for my son this week? How would I heat the house? Tears ran down my face as I rocked on my chair, feeling helpless and abandoned.

Someone walked towards me. It was Nuala, a girl I'd met before through the meditation circle. She held out a £50 note in her hand, saying, 'I'd like you to take this.'

'I can't take that Nuala, it's too much!' I cried back at her.

She sat down beside me, took my hand and said, 'Let me tell you a story.'

Nuala told me how, just a month earlier, she'd been up in Dublin at another event. When she went to pay for her room, she discovered her purse was missing. She was shocked, just like me, and wondering what on earth to do when a man, a complete stranger, came up to her, proffering a £50 note and said, 'I'd like you to take this.'

Nuala explained that she was only passing it on now to someone else who needed it.

Her story made all the difference, and I was able to accept her gift with a hug and more tears, feeling truly grateful. I started to think that perhaps having an open heart wasn't just about being able to give, but also about being able to receive.

A few days later, I was on my way to a meeting and stopped at my local shop to buy biscuits for the tea-break. In my hand I had a £20 note – all that was left of Nuala's gift. As I walked in I heard a distraught woman telling the shopkeeper how she had lost a sum of money and didn't know how she would manage to pay her rent. I looked at the crisp note in my hand, looked at her and said, 'Oh, I think this must be for you.'

Well, she looked at me as if I was quite mad! 'Please take it,' I insisted. She backed away from me, suspicious.

'Please, listen to me. Let me tell you a story,' I said.

I told her about the Green Lady I'd seen in Galway on St Brigit's Day, about my purse being stolen, about Nuala's generosity and her own story. Tears welled up in the woman's eyes. As she reached out towards me I put the £20 note in her hand, then held her as she wept. 'No one has ever been so kind to me,' she said.

'It's not me that is giving to you,' I said. 'I'm only passing it on.'

A true story

Games

Green Lady

The green lady of spring is asleep under the blanket of snow. She needs to be awoken.

One player is chosen as the green lady. She lies on the ground, under a blanket. The others slowly circle around her chanting:

'Green lady, green lady, your breakfast is ready.
Green lady, green lady, your dinner is ready.
Green lady, green lady, your supper is ready.
Green lady, green lady, your house is on fire!'

The green lady then leaps up and chases the others. The first to be caught becomes the new green lady and lies under the blanket.

Candlemas, 2 February

This is a celebration of the ritual cleansing or purification of Mary after the birth of her son Jesus, when Mary was to present her child in the temple according to the Jewish tradition.

According to an old story, Mary was feeling a little uncomfortable about the attention that this public appearance would bring. She had, after all, not yet married when she became pregnant. So Brigit walked ahead of Mary as she brought Jesus into the temple, wearing a spectacular crown of lights – made of a harrow with a lighted candle on each point! Thus Brigit distracted the attention of the onlookers, and Mary was able to fulfil her duties without embarrassment.

Brigit wore another crown of lights as she danced to draw the attention of Herod's soldiers away from Mary and her child and so helped them to escape on their flight to Egypt.

Candlemas day comes after Brigit's day because Mary wanted to honour her good friend Brigit for saving the life of her baby Jesus.

Candlemas is celebrated as a festival of lights. Candles are brought as gifts to the churches and blessed as a reminder of the birth of the light. People also bring their own candles to be blessed for use at home. At Candlemas people used to put lighted candles around beehives. Today the crib is finally put away until next year.

If Candlemas day was bright, farmers thought that the rest of February would be cold and wet.

If you see a hedgehog on Candlemas day you should observe his behaviour. If he stays out of his burrow then the weather will be fine, but if he goes back to sleep, you can expect more wintry weather.

I have heard a rumour that St Patrick expelled the snakes from Ireland at Candlemas!

How Brigit helped Mary to escape the wrath of Herod

*L*ONG AGO, *when Jesus was just a baby, King Herod heard a prophecy that a child who had been born recently in his city would become the greatest king the earth had ever known. King Herod was jealous.* **He** *wanted to be remembered as the greatest king of this country! He became afraid for his throne and wondered how he could safeguard his position.*

At last he came to a decision – he would slay every boy child in the city less than three months old. That would solve the problem once and for all! So he set sentries on the city's gates and soldiers watched all the roads and bridges leading from the city. Tomorrow at dawn he would begin his search for the infants.

Brigit tended the fires in the castle and heard rumours of a planned slaughter. She came running to warn her good friend Mary. 'Oh, Mary, there is terrible news. The king plans to kill every baby boy in the city. No one can escape. He has put guards on all the gates!'

'But how can I save my little one?' Mary gasped. Brigit took her trembling hand and said, 'I will think of some way to get you past the sentries and out of the city. Now, let us find a plan.'

The two women sat in silence, thinking hard, while the baby Jesus gurgled and smiled.

'I know what! You must get all your goods together and be ready to leave at first light. I will dress myself as a fool and distract the guards away from their posts. You must head south and cross the river by the golden bridge. I must go now and prepare myself for the morning. Goodbye, my dear friend, let us pray we meet again.'

When Joseph returned from his business, Mary told him the news. He agreed, yes, they must leave in the morning.

Next morning just as the sun was rising, a loud crashing and banging could be heard near the city gates. Mary peeped outside and saw a crazy woman, dressed all in straw with a belt of lights and a crown of candles on her head, dancing and beating a drum. The crazy woman danced in circles up the road, banging her drum and blowing on a whistle.

The guards jumped with surprise at the shrill whistle and ran towards the strange dancer, calling, 'You must be quiet, woman, or you will wake the whole city. Good folks deserve a decent rest.'

But the woman kept dancing, moving off towards the market square and the guards followed her, leaving their posts unattended.

Mary saw her chance. She ran through the unguarded gates and south towards the river, but there were soldiers on the bridge also!

'Where are you going so early in the day?' the guards asked.

'My home is a good distance from here and I must start early if I am to reach there by nightfall.'

'What is that you carry on your back?'

'It is a little lamb I thought to rear as a pet. It was a gift from a friend.'

'I don't trust her,' said the first guard, seizing Mary and pulling aside her mantle. But there on her back was a lamb with its feet lightly bound together.

'Look, it's as she said,' said the other soldier.

'Let her go on her way.'

Mary walked on until she was well away from the city, then she sat in the shade of a fig tree and lifted the baby Jesus from the lambskin on her back. And when she had rested and the babe had supped his fill, she walked on south towards safety.

Some weeks later Brigit joined her there and the two women wept with joy, giving thanks to God for saving them all. Then Mary gave Brigit a present of a feast day in her own name, and said, 'Your feast day shall come before my day, Brigit, from now until the end of the world.'

And so it has been ever since, and as candles were in the plan that led Mary and her son to safety, so Candlemas is the name of Mary's feast.

Candle making

Beeswax and tallow are the traditional materials for candle making. Tallow, being rendered from animal fats, has an unpleasant smell as it burns, while beeswax has a sweet honey-like scent. Beeswax is expensive and can be difficult to find in large enough quantities for making candles.

For the little, shaped candles (see below), you could melt down the stumps of old candles. For larger candles, you will have to buy white paraffin wax and stearin, a white powder whose addition helps the candle to set well and to burn evenly. Candle moulds are available from art and craft suppliers and come in many shapes and sizes, but you can still make candles even if you don't have these. You can use well-washed yoghurt pots or tin cans as moulds. You can also make candles in walnut shells, eggshells or you can try dipping candles. You can even make candles by pouring melted wax into a hollow in the earth!

Little shaped candles

You will need:
Small quantity of white wax
Coloured wax crayons
Cotton string
Small pastry or playdough cutters
Aluminium foil or an old baking tray
Double boiler or two saucepans

Method:
Melt the wax. You can change the colour by adding small shavings from coloured crayons to the hot wax.
Dip lengths of string into the melted wax and remove for the wicks. Allow to dry straight.
Rub a little washing-up liquid on the inside of the pastry cutters, so that the wax won't stick. Place the cutters on a sheet of aluminium foil or an old baking tray.

Pour a little wax into each cutter.
While the wax is still liquid, place a 2.5cm / 1 inch long wick into the centre of each little candle.
Leave to cool and set. Remove from the moulds when hard.

Candle dipping

You will need:
Wax
Wick
A little piece of lead

Method:
Melt wax. Attach the lead weight to the wick and dip the wick into the melted wax. Allow it to cool.
Dip the wick into the melted wax and allow to cool again. Repeat the dipping and cooling until you have built up layer upon layer of wax and your candle is a pleasing shape.
Remove the weight by cutting through the candle and wick with a knife or scissors warmed in hot water.

Rush light

A rush light is a sort of candle that uses the soft white spongy pith from the rush as a wick. The type of rushes you need grow abundantly on wet land.

You will need:
Rushes *(Juncus effusus* or *Juncus conglomeratus)*
Wax or white hard vegetable fat
Tin can for melting wax or fat

Method:
Pick rushes and allow to dry out in the sun.
Peel away the green skin of the rush on one side to expose the white pith. Leave enough skin to support the pith.
Melt wax or vegetable fat in a tin can. Do not let it boil.
Dip each rush one by one into the melted wax and allow to cool and solidify. Dip each rush again three or four times, allowing it to harden between dips.
Use as a candle.

Earth candle

You will need:
Wax
Wick
A pencil or stick
Sand

Method:
Dig a hole in the ground. Fill it with sand and then make a hole within the sand.
Melt wax in a double boiler, or small pot inside a larger pot of boiling water.
Prepare a wick by dipping a length of string the depth of the hole plus 5cm / 2 inches into the melted wax.
Attach a weight to one end of the wick, and tie the other end around a pencil or a thin stick.
Lower the wick into the hole and let the pencil support it on the sides of the hole.

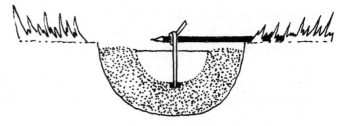

Pour melted wax into the hole and wait for it to harden.
Dig up the candle, invert it and dust off the excess soil.

St Valentine's Day, 14 February

Valentine's Day seems to be becoming a bigger event in Ireland as time goes on. It falls during the time when matchmakers were traditionally busy trying to arrange marriages that would take place before the prohibitions of Lent.

Some say that on Valentine's Day the birds choose their mates. From my own observations, I'd say that on this day the frogs choose theirs! They are often to be seen in watery places, laying eggs, so this is probably a good time to go out in search of frogspawn. And if you were to kiss one, well, who knows what might happen!

Bishop Valentine of Rome was martyred in the 3rd century on 14 February, the eve of the ancient Roman feast of Lupercalia. During this feast, names of young men and women were placed in a box and chosen at random to be sweethearts.

Today's sweethearts send cards and flowers, declaring their devotion to the beloved on Valentine's Day. The tradition is that the cards, bearing motifs of hearts, flowers and birds, are sent anonymously or signed: 'From a secret admirer'.

Things to make

Valentine card

You will need:
White card
Gold paper
Paper doily
Red paper or card
Scissors or craft knife
Glue stick

Method:
Cut card to desired size and fold in half.
Cut a circle from gold card and dab of glue in the centre.
Cut a lacy circle from the doily and glue this to the gold card, placing it carefully.
Cut a heart from the red card. Put a dab of glue on the back of the heart and place it centrally on the doily.
Glue the whole assembly onto the centre of the card and allow to dry.
Open the card and write your message inside.

Heart brooch

You will need:
Small piece of red satin or velvet
Sheep's wool or cotton wool
Thread
Small safety pin

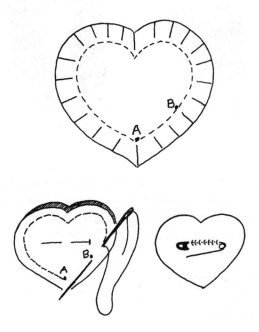

Method:
Copy the pattern onto your fabric and cut out two pieces.

Sew together with right sides facing, leaving an opening at A-B.

Turn right side out and stuff with sheep's wool.

Sew the non-opening side of the safety pin onto the centre of one side of the badge.

Now you can wear your heart on your sleeve (or on your jumper), or give it away to someone you love.

Heart baskets

You will need:
Red paper 5cm x 23cm / 2 inches x 9 inches
White paper 5cm x 23cm / 2 inches x 9 inches
Scissors and glue
Coloured thread

Method:
Place the two papers one on top of the other and fold in half.

Cut as shown. Place at right angles to each other, forming a heart shape. Weave the strips over and under as shown in diagram.

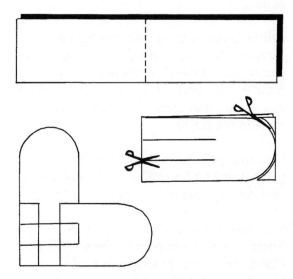

Use coloured thread to make a handle and hang from a spring branch or place a little gift in the basket and give it to your Valentine.

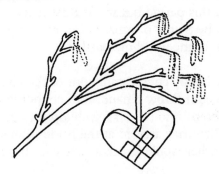

Shrove Tuesday

Shrove Tuesday was traditionally the last chance to use up all the stored milk, butter, cheese and eggs before the beginning of the Lenten fast. These are the ingredients needed to make the pancakes that give this day its other name of Pancake Tuesday. Pancakes are still made in almost every house in Ireland on this day.

An unmarried girl's skill in tossing a pancake could determine whether she would marry that year. If she caught the tossed pancake without a wrinkle, then her prospects were good.

A little piece of meat from the Shrove Tuesday meal was pinned to the ceiling or placed within the chimney until Easter Sunday. This practice was to bring good luck and ensure that there would be no lack of meat in the house.

One strange belief was that if you were to lick a lizard on Shrove Tuesday, this would give your tongue the power to heal burns.

The days before and including Shrove Tuesday were most popular for weddings. Matchmakers were busy from Little Christmas onwards – 6 January – arranging marriages.

It may be that marriage was forbidden during Lent, so people rushed to marry before this period began. At least there would be plenty of milk, butter and eggs to use up in the wedding feast!

As the happy couple came out of the church they would throw a handful of copper and silver coins into the air for children to gather up. When they arrived at the bride's house, her mother would break a cake over her head and then the party would begin, with singing, dancing and a visit from the straw-boys (men dressed in suits and masks of straw) who each claimed a dance with the bride.

Festive food

Pancakes

Ingredients:
8 oz / 225g flour
1 pint / 570ml milk
Pinch salt
4 eggs
Lemon juice and sugar to taste

Method:

Sift the flour and salt into a bowl. Beat the eggs with the milk in another bowl. Add half of the liquid to the flour and beat well. Beat in the rest of the egg and milk, beating well.

Leave the mixture to stand for an hour or two.

Heat a little oil in a heavy frying pan. Add 1/4 cup of the pancake batter and tip the pan until the mixture has spread evenly over the pan.

Keep the pan moving over the heat, so that the pancake doesn't burn or stick to the pan.

When the first side is cooked, flip the pancake over and cook the other side.

Remove to a plate and sprinkle with lemon juice and sugar to taste. Roll the pancake up and eat it with your hands.

You can keep pancakes warm by piling them one on top of the other and putting them in a warm oven.

Stuffed pancakes

Ingredients:

As above, adding a little more milk to make a slightly runnier batter

Sweet filling:

Grated apple
Pinch cinnamon
Teaspoon honey
Lemon juice

Savoury filling:

Finely grated carrot
Finely grated cheddar cheese
Pinch mixed herbs

Method:

Prepare the filling by mixing in a in a bowl. Heat a little sunflower oil in a heavy frying pan. Pour two tablespoons of batter into the pan and spread it thinly and evenly. Cook until the first side is not quite ready – it will still appear a little wet in places.

Place a tablespoon of the stuffing (either sweet or savoury) on one half of the pancake and fold the other half over to make a half moon shape. Press down the 'lid' to seal it.

Cook for a few minutes more on each side. Put on a plate and serve.

Serve the savoury pancakes with a little salad.

Serve the sweet pancakes with natural yoghurt.

Drop scones

Ingredients:

8 oz / 225g flour
4 tsp baking powder
1 beaten egg
1 dessertspoon golden syrup
8 fl oz / 216ml milk

Method:

Heat a heavy frying pan. Sift flour and baking powder into a bowl. Make a well in the centre and pour in the egg, syrup and milk.

Whisk well, making sure to break up any lumps, until the batter looks like thick cream. If it is too thick add a little more milk.

Put a little oil in the pan and drop in spoonfuls of batter. When the bubbles that appear on the top of the pancake burst, it is time to turn it over and cook the other side.

Serve with butter and jam or honey.

Lent

Ash Wednesday is the day after Shrove Tuesday, and is also the first day of Lent. Those who go to church receive a cross of ashes on their foreheads.

In older times people were expected to abstain from all animal fats during Lent. This meant no eggs, butter, milk or meat, so the people ate simple meals like porridge, with black tea for breakfast; and potatoes, herring and seaweed for dinner. This restraint was expected of all but the poorest of folk, who were advised to eat whatever they could get.

In the 19th century the custom changed so that only Ash Wednesday and Good Friday were strictly observed fasts. There was a prohibition on dancing and singing during Lent. Visiting friends was frowned upon, as were card games; and still today many people decide not to visit the pub during this period.

The first Sunday of Lent was known as Chalk Sunday or Puss Sunday. Boys and girls would make a chalk mark on the clothes of anyone eligible but still unmarried. Those who did not marry were thought to be unhappy about this state of affairs, and to have a puss, or scowl, on their faces.

Nowadays, many people choose to give something up for Lent. This can be a habit, or something like chocolate or sweets. You could also choose to take up some spiritual discipline during this time.

One curious exception to the abstention from meat, was the eating of the barnacle goose. Many people believed that these birds grew from shellfish rather than eggs and so thought it was permissible to eat them during Lent.

The Vision of MacConglinne

KING CATHAL of Munster was known as a fine and fair king, a champion in battle and a sound giver of laws. That is, he was, until a strange and hungry beast came to dwell within his belly. Since then the king had been hungry day and night with an appetite that could not be sated. As soon as he woke in the morning he would eat a whole pig, even before he was dressed, and follow that with a whole cow and forty cakes of wheaten meal, washed down with a barrel of ale. That was his breakfast, and for his dinner, he ate – no, I have not room on this page to tell you all he put into his kingly mouth.

For three years the king fed the huge appetite of the beast in his belly, and the kingdom of Munster was suffering, strained and hungry from the king's greed.

The story of King Cathal's voracious appetite spread throughout the land, and at last reached the ear of MacConglinne, a young scholar, as he laboured at his scribing in Armagh. When he heard of the king's strange condition he decided to leave his books and try his fortune with a cure for the mysterious ailment.

He rose early, dressed in his white cloak, walked sunwise around the house bidding farewell to his tutors and set his foot to the road south. Many days he walked and nights he spent in rich men's halls, entertaining them with tales for his supper.

At last he came to the house of Pichan where again he told his tales and as usual, everyone laughed and delighted in his stories. All but Pichan, who did not smile at all. 'What ails ye?' MacConglinne asked his host.

'Tomorrow King Cathal comes to visit my house and I fear he will leave our stores empty, such is his greed. He has ordered for his welcome forty barrels of apples and forty more of wheaten cakes. I can only hope he will not stay too long. We have barely enough to last ourselves the winter.'

'Hmm,' said MacConglinne, 'I may be able to help.'

A trumpet sounded and the sound of hooves proclaimed the entry of King Cathal and his retinue into Pichan's tower. Before he had even washed and changed from his travelling clothes, the king reached for the apple barrels and began to cram handfuls of the fruits into his mouth. Pichan watched with an open mouth and sorrowful eyes as his king stuffed his harvest into his mouth without grace or care.

Just then MacConglinne came forth before the king and picked up a stone. He put the stone into his own mouth and began to grind his teeth upon it.

'What has made you so mad, scholar, that you chew on a stone?' the king asked.

'Sire, I cannot bear to see you dine alone, so I thought to join you,' MacConglinne replied.

King Cathal tossed an apple towards him, saying, 'Here boy, you shame me. Join me then and eat.' This was the first time in three years that the king had shown any shame or any generosity.

'I thank you sire. Now may I ask you one more boon?' asked the scholar. 'Ask away, boy, for surely I will grant it.' 'I ask this sire. That you will agree to fast with me this night.'

Since the king had already given his royal word he had no choice but to agree, and despite the hungry beast's roars, he fasted that night.

In the morning MacConglinne set a fire with fine oak wood and called for a juicy side of bacon and a tender corned beef. He called for golden honeycomb dripping onto a silver plate and crystal salt in a silver bowl. He set up a spit and began to roast the fine meats over the fire. When the scent of the roasting filled the hall, he called for stout rope and six strong men.

'Hold the king fast and bind him to his chair,' he ordered.

The warriors held Cathal down and fastened him with rope and twine and chains so that he could not move. Then MacConglinne sat himself before the king and took out his knife. Carefully he carved the roasted meat, dipping each slice in honey and salt. He passed each morsel before the king's nose then put it into his own mouth and ate it.

As the king struggled against his ropes, MacConglinne said to him, 'Last night a vision came to me, and I must share it with you.'

'I saw a lake of new milk in a plain. By this lake stood a fine house and its thatch was made of butter, held down by boiled puddings. The doorposts were a soft yellow custard and the window frames of creamy curds. The roof beams were sausages, the beds slices of bacon. It was a truly magnificent house, and its store was packed with delicious and wonderful foods.

'But as I stood before this house, I had no appetite to eat of it at all. A voice told me to travel across the new milk lake to the druid doctor who would restore my desire for food.

'I rowed in a coracle of beef with oars of venison, passing oceans of broth and seas of porridge, rivers of ale and islands of cheese, until I came to the foot of a mountain of yellow butter. There stood the hut of the druid doctor, and it was wonderful to behold, standing behind a fence of carrots topped with soured cream, and before a forest of broccoli. When the druid asked what ailed me, I told him that I wished I might have appetite to eat these wonderful foods around me, but that alas, I could not eat.

'The good doctor prescribed for me a cure, saying, "Go home now and warm yourself before a fire of oak logs. Prepare three times nine morsels, each the size of an egg. In each of these put eight types of grain, among them wheat and barley, oats and rye, and with these, eight condiments and eight sauces. And when you have this done, take a drop of milk, as much as 20 men would drink, and pour this down your throat. This will cure your disease. Go now in the name of cheese, and may juicy bacon protect you, may yellow cream protect

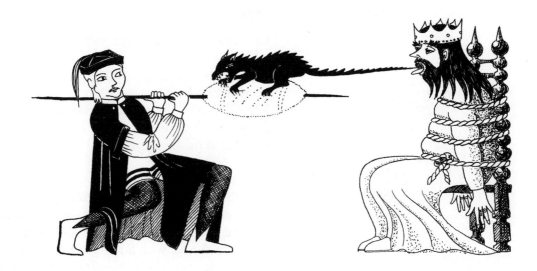

you, and may the cauldron full of soup protect you."'

As MacConglinne told the king of his vision, the hungry beast could be seen emerging from King Cathal's mouth and licking his lips. MacConglinne picked up the spit and brought it close to the king, who by now so longed to eat them whole – meat and wood and all. The scholar stepped back, drawing the spit an arm's length away from Cathal's face, then another step back.

Suddenly the hungry beast leapt from King Cathal's mouth onto the spit and began to eat with a fury. MacConglinne dashed the spit into the fire and ordered all to leave the hall. As the beast burned in the fire, the king was cured of his craving.

King Cathal was most generous in his reward to the young scholar, granting him a cow from each farm and a sheep from each house in Munster.

Now MacConglinne sits at the right hand of the king and carves the meat in his hall, and there he continues to entertain all with his tales.

Things to make and do

Spring cleaning inside and out

Springtime is the time to clear out cupboards and drawers, dust off the shelves and give away or throw out anything you no longer need. A good guideline is: if it's not beautiful or useful, I don't need it any more.

This is also a very appropriate time to undertake a cleansing diet. Herbs such as dandelions and nettles are great spring tonics. Add dandelion leaves to a salad. Nettles make a very good cleansing and iron-rich tea, and a wonderful soup when combined with potatoes and onions. Identifying nettles will not be a problem, most people have been stung by them at some time. You might want to wear gloves when you pick the nettles to avoid the sting, although it is said that nettle stings will protect you against arthritis. Pick only young shoots or the top parts of older plants, as other parts are rather coarse.

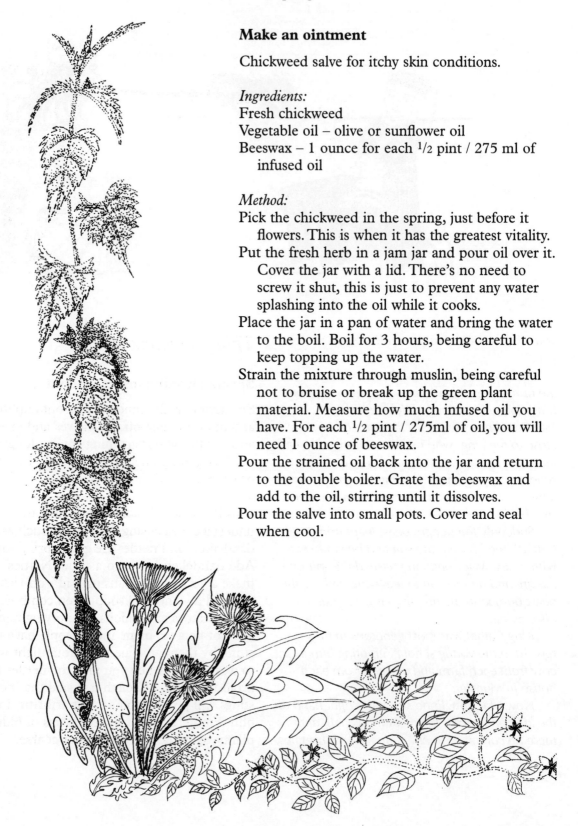

Make an ointment

Chickweed salve for itchy skin conditions.

Ingredients:
Fresh chickweed
Vegetable oil – olive or sunflower oil
Beeswax – 1 ounce for each $1/2$ pint / 275 ml of
   infused oil

Method:
Pick the chickweed in the spring, just before it
   flowers. This is when it has the greatest vitality.
Put the fresh herb in a jam jar and pour oil over it.
   Cover the jar with a lid. There's no need to
   screw it shut, this is just to prevent any water
   splashing into the oil while it cooks.
Place the jar in a pan of water and bring the water
   to the boil. Boil for 3 hours, being careful to
   keep topping up the water.
Strain the mixture through muslin, being careful
   not to bruise or break up the green plant
   material. Measure how much infused oil you
   have. For each $1/2$ pint / 275ml of oil, you will
   need 1 ounce of beeswax.
Pour the strained oil back into the jar and return
   to the double boiler. Grate the beeswax and
   add to the oil, stirring until it dissolves.
Pour the salve into small pots. Cover and seal
   when cool.

Festive food

Nettle soup

Ingredients:
5 oz / 140g nettles
1 large onion
10 oz / 275g potatoes
1 tbsp olive oil or 1 oz / 25g butter
1¹/₂ pint / 84ml water
Vegetable stock cube
Sea salt and black pepper
¹/₄ pint / 138ml milk or cream – optional

Method:
Gather your nettles and wash in cold water.
Peel and chop the onion and fry softly in olive oil or butter in a large saucepan.
Scrub the potatoes and cut into slices 1cm / ¹/₂ inch thick. Add to the onions and stir until coated in oil.
Put a lid on the pan and allow to steam until the potatoes begin to soften. Add the water, stock cube and chopped nettles and bring to the boil.
Reduce the heat and simmer for a few minutes. Liquidize the soup in a blender or food processor.
At this stage you can stir in the milk or cream, although the soup is just as tasty without. Add salt and pepper to taste.

Nettle champ

Ingredients:
Mashed potato
¹/₂ pint / 275ml milk
1 cup nettles
1 oz / 25g butter
Salt and pepper

Method:
Simmer the nettles in milk for ten minutes.
Pour the milk and nettle mixture into the potatoes and mash together with the butter.
Add salt and pepper to taste.

How to behave among strangers

Be not too wise, nor too foolish
be not too conceited, nor too diffident,
be not too haughty, nor too humble,
be not too talkative, nor too silent,
be not too hard, nor too feeble.

If you be too wise, one will expect too much of you;
if you be too foolish, you will be deceived;
if you be too conceited, you will be thought vexatious;
if you be too talkative, you will not be heeded;
if you be too silent, you will not be regarded;
if you be too hard, you will be broken;
if you be too feeble, you will be crushed.

from *The Instructions of Cormac,* translation Kuno Meyer, Ancient Irish Poetry, 1913

St Patrick's Day, 17 March

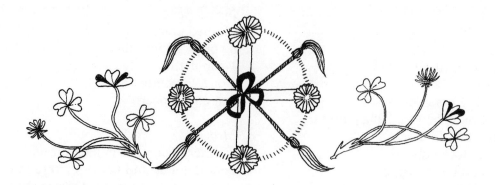

This was not one of the old festivals in Ireland, but is now celebrated on a grand scale throughout the country and abroad, wherever there is an expatriate Irish community. St Patrick's Day parades are held in most towns, large or small. Schools, clubs and organisations parade in fancy dress on foot or on a lorry float through the main streets of the town. There is usually a prize awarded to the best display.

St Patrick's day was a welcome exemption from the Lenten fast, when people could eat and drink as they wished and could go out and make merry with friends and neighbours. There was a tradition for men to go to the local pub and drink the *póta Padraig* or St Patrick's pot.

In older times people wore an emblem of the saint on his day, a St Patrick's cross made of paper or cloth. Today many people pin a bunch of shamrock to their coat on the day.

A custom associated with this day is the 'drowning of the shamrock'. At the end of the day the shamrock that has been worn on the coat or hat is put into the last glass of ale or punch. After a toast was made and a little of the drink taken, the shamrock was fished out again and thrown over the left shoulder.

As St Patrick's day is so close to the spring equinox, it was often considered as the middle of spring, and farmers would plant their main potato crop around this time, and by Good Friday at the latest.

The week leading up to St Patrick's day is known as *Seachtain na Gaeilge* or Irish Week. People are encouraged to use the Irish language as much as possible. No matter how little Irish they have they are encouraged to use it and speak as *Gaeilge*.

The life of St Patrick

Patrick was born Magonus Sucratus Patricius in Northern England in the 4th century CE to a comfortable family. His father was a deacon, a Roman, and his mother was British. When he was sixteen he was captured by slave traders, sold to an Irish farmer and became a shepherd in the hills of County Antrim. Whilst minding his master's sheep, he remembered the prayers he had paid little attention to as a child. He is said to have prayed up to 100 prayers a day, both by day and by night, on the hillside, in the forest, in rain and in sun, in snow or in frost. After six years as a slave, Patrick heard a voice telling him to return to his native land. The voice said that a ship to bring him home awaited him. Patrick walked 200 miles till he found the promised boat and journeyed home. After being reunited with his family, he travelled to Gaul to study for the priesthood. All this time he was aware of 'the voice of the Irish' calling him to return to Ireland.

In 432 he returned to Ireland as a bishop and took it upon himself to convert the natives to Christianity. He established a church at Saul near Strangford Lough and later at Armagh. Amongst his famous deeds are the use of the three-leafed shamrock to explain the nature of the Trinity.

He lit the Paschal fire on the hill of Slane before the King Laoghaire lit the sacred Bealtaine fire on the hill of Tara. When challenged over this Patrick proved himself to be a man channelling a power greater than the druids. He cursed the rushes that used to prick him as he walked and that is why their tips are brown.

Towards the end of his life he spent forty days and nights fasting in the wilderness on top of Croagh Patrick in County Mayo. This inspired the pilgrimage that takes place on Croagh Padraig on Reek Sunday (last Sunday in July), when many walk up the mountain's stony sides with bare feet.

Aengus, a prince of Munster, had heard Patrick speak many times and he longed to be baptised into the Christian faith. Patrick agreed to baptise him and a great crowd gathered around to witness the occasion. Patrick took out his book, but found that his crosier was getting in the way of his finding the appropriate verse. He stuck the pointed

end of his crosier into the ground so that his hands were free to perform the rite of baptism, but did not notice that he had pushed it right through Aengus' foot! Aengus made no sound, nor did he flinch, so Patrick was none the wiser about the prince's wounded foot and continued with the baptism. Aengus' face grew a little pale as Patrick poured the water over his bowed head and spoke the words of the rite. When the business was complete Patrick turned to take up his crosier and was horrified to discover that he had pierced the prince's foot!

As Patrick apologised, he asked the prince why he had not cried out. Aengus replied that he thought that this must be a part of the ceremony and he did not wish to appear weak before his people by crying out in pain, adding, 'You tell us that Christ shed his blood for me. I am not afraid to suffer a little pain on his behalf.'

The Last of the Fianna

LONG AGO when the land of Ireland was full of heroes, Finn MacCool led a band of warriors, the Fianna. The Fianna were known for their proud deeds. Great were their adventures, and the bards told of their prowess in halls throughout the length and breadth of the land. It would be hard to find a body who did not know the name of Finn MacCool.

Finn had many sons, among them one who was born while his mother had taken the form of a deer. She named him Oisín, which means little deer. Oisín grew to be a strong, handsome man and a fine warrior and rode with the Fianna in many battles.

After the battle of Gowra, when the Fianna were defeated, Finn led his men wearily homeward. As they rode a track through a forest, Finn spied a golden hind that turned to face them and then ran off through the trees. The prospect of a hunt restored the spirits of the battle-weary Fianna and so they gave chase. When they reached a clearing the deer halted for one moment, shook itself and suddenly there before them was a girl on a white horse. The maiden wore a white gown that seemed to shimmer with all the colours of the rainbow. Down her back hung long honey-coloured hair, bound with gold beads and cords. Her face shone with a radiant light.

'Men of the Fianna, cease your chase!' she called, in a voice like a clear bell. 'I am Niamh of the Golden Hair. My father is king of the land under wave, Tir na Nog, the land of the ever young. I have come from Tir na Nog seeking a husband'.

The warriors could not take their eyes from her, so great was her beauty. They nudged each other in the ribs, wondering which of them would be the lucky man. She spoke again, 'Finn MacCool, I would marry your son Oisín. Long have I watched him from afar and my heart is full of love for him. I ask your permission to take him with me to Tir na Nog.'

Oisín stepped forward and took the maiden's hand. 'Come with me, Oisín, to Tir na Nog. There you shall live in splendour. Never shall you want for aught, nor will you ever grow old. Come with me my love and stay forever young.'

Finn stepped between the two saying, 'I counsel you my son, do not listen to the fairy woman. She has set an enchantment on you. Stay with us, your comrades. Live out your life of glory and die a hero's death in battle.'

'No, father. Never have I known a maid so fair, but in my dreams. Farewell to you, my father, and my friends.'

Oisín climbed up behind Niamh on the white horse while Finn called out in anguish, 'Oisín, beloved son, I beg you. Never will we meet again!' Without a backward glance the two rode off towards the West. Down to the pebbly shore they rode and out over the crests of the waves. Over the sea and beyond the foam they rode, passing over submerged palaces where bells still rang and fishes swam through the ornamental arches, till at last they reached Niamh's father's palace.

Jumping down from the horse with wondrous grace, Niamh greeted him, 'Father, here is the man I would marry. Oisín, son of the hero Finn MacCool.'

The king opened wide his arms to embrace Oisín and welcome him to Tir na Nog. And so the two were married and three children, bonny and fair, were born and all were happy and content.

Time has no meaning in Tir na Nog, but three hundred years had passed in the world of men when Oisín felt a sickness in his heart for home. 'I long to see the faces of my father and my friends once more. I must return to Ireland.'

'You cannot go, my love. You will not find there what you seek. Ireland is not as it was. I beg you, do not go, for you may never return to me.'

'I will come back to you I promise, for our good horse surely knows the way. It would gladden my heart to see my old home again.'

'I cannot stop you, if go you must, but promise me one thing. Do not place one foot upon the earth. Stay on the horse, for while you remain on him you are still part of Tir na Nog. Step onto the land and there you must remain and will be lost to me forever.'

Oisín rode the white horse over the waves till he spied the green land of Ireland once more. He rode up over the pebbly shore and along the old familiar roads, but could find no trace of the strongholds of the Fianna. As he rode on, it seemed to him that everything looked smaller and duller than in his memory.

A crowd gathered at the roadside looked aghast as he rode up. A little child, from behind his mother's skirts said, 'Mammy, is that man a giant?'

Oisín called, 'Good people, where must I go to find Finn MacCool?'

'To his grave, if you can find it!' the people told him. 'He's been dead three hundred years!'

Then another spoke, 'But sir, seeing as you're so strong and all, maybe you can help us out. A great stone has fallen and our friends are trapped beneath.'

Oisín reached down for the stone, leaning over in his saddle, and with one hand he lifted the stone slab. As he tossed it through the air, he lost his balance and leaning over, put down one foot to steady himself. A great weariness came over him. The moment his foot touched the

earth his skin grew taut and dry. His hair turned first grey, then white and then fell from his head. His eye began to grow dim and his hearing to fade. Too late, he remembered Niamh's warning, and now he knew he would never see her again.

The crowd gathered around the old man who lay on the ground and helped him to sit up. One man called, 'Fetch Patrick. He surely can help this poor man.'

They brought to him a man in a plain brown robe, around whose neck hung a small silver cross. From a basket Patrick took a lump of bread. He dipped it in a cup of water and held it to Oisín's lips, saying, 'Eat, old man, and then we can talk.'

For three months Oisín stayed with Patrick in his little stone cell. Each night Oisín told stories of the old days and the adventures of the Fianna, and Patrick wrote these down in his book. By day Patrick told stories of the new god and the two argued long and laughed aplenty, becoming firm friends. And so at last, as he lay dying, Oisín, the last of the Fianna, asked Patrick to baptise him into the new faith.

St Patrick's breastplate

This beautiful prayer for protection is also known as *The Deer's Cry.* There is a story that when Patrick and his followers were ambushed, he spoke this prayer and instantly his party were concealed and all that the attackers saw was a group of deer in the mist.

Here is an extract from the prayer:

I arise today
Through the strength of Heaven:
Light of Sun,
Radiance of Moon,
Splendour of Fire,
Speed of Lightning,
Swiftness of Wind,
Depth of Sea,
Stability of Earth,
Firmness of Rock.

Christ with me, Christ before me, Christ behind me,
Christ in me, Christ beneath me, Christ above me,
Christ on my right, Christ on my left
Christ when I lie down, Christ when I sit down, Christ when I arise,
Christ in the heart of every man that thinks of me,
Christ in the mouth of every one who speaks of me.

From *St Patrick's Breastplate,* translated by Kuno Meyer, from *Ancient Irish Poetry*

St Patrick's hymn

I bind unto myself today
the strong name of the Trinity
By invocation of the same,
The Three in One and One in Three.

Festive food

Shamrock rolls

Ingredients:
Bread dough (made with yeast and milk)
Cup cake tin

Method:
Break dough into small pieces and roll these
    into balls about 2cm / ³/₄ inch in diameter.
Grease the cup cake tins.
Put three little balls in each tin with a small
    amount of butter in between each piece
    and leave until they have doubled in size.
Bake at Gas mark 5 (350°F / 180°C) for 20
    minutes.

Things to make

Pin-on shamrock

You will need:
15cm / 6 inch square of green felt
Needle and thread
Sheep's wool or cotton wool
Scissors
Safety pin

Method:
Copy the pattern onto the felt and cut out
    two shamrocks.
Sew around the edges with blanket stitch,
    leaving a gap at A-B.
Insert the sheep's or cotton wool as stuffing
    and then sew up the gap.
Sew the safety pin to the back of the
    shamrock.

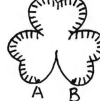 

Mothering Sunday

Fourth Sunday in Lent

Originally a day to honour 'Mother Church', this later developed into a day to honour our own mothers. Servants and apprentices who lived away from home had the day off work to visit their mothers. They would bring gifts of flowers and cake.

Children often take over their mother's (or in these politically correct days, their primary care-giver's) tasks for the day, and sometimes even bring breakfast in bed! Nowadays many families go out for a meal on Mothering Sunday.

Daffodils are usually in bloom around this time, and a bunch of flowers or a small token gift in a hand-made box makes a lovely Mother's Day present to put on a beautifully laid table.

Things to make

Mother's Day gift box

You will need:
Thin card or heavy paper
Glue stick
Scissors
A round or square cake of soap
Coloured tissue paper

Method:
To make a box 5cm / 2 inches square, you will need to start with a 20cm / 8 inch square. Cut a square of card. Make two folds from corner to corner as shown in figure 1. Crease well and then open out.

figure 1

Fold each corner in towards the centre point (figure 2). Crease well and open out again. There are now 6 fold lines on the card (figure 3).

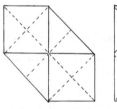

figure 2   *figure 3*

Fold the bottom corner up to the centre of the top fold line (figure 4). Crease and open out, then repeat with the other three corners. There are now 10 creases on the card (figure 5).

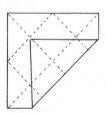   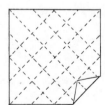

figure 4   *figure 5*

Now fold each corner up to the bottom
crease and unfold again. The card is now
covered with a grid of creases. There are
two small triangles (shaded in figure 6) on
each edge of the square. Cut these out.

figure 6

Now draw a petal shape on each of the four
corners marked X. Cut around the petals
(figure 7).

figure 7   *figure 8*

Make four cuts as shown (figure 8).
Fold to form a box with the central four
squares as its base. Glue flaps A onto
squares marked B and hold in place until
glue is dry.
Fold the petal back.
Rumple the tissue paper and place in the
box. Lay the soap on the tissue and close
the box.
To close box, overlap the left-hand corner of
each flap over the right hand corner of the
next flap.
Lift the petals up to form a flower shape.

Posy of flowers

You will need:
A small bunch of flowers
A few leaves, especially ferns
Kitchen paper towels
Aluminium foil
Ribbon
Paper doily

Method:
Arrange the flowers with the largest to the
middle, smaller flowers outside. Place the
ferns outside of the flowers.
Cut the stalks to the same length.
Moisten the kitchen paper and wrap it
around the bottom of the stalks.
Cut out the centre of the paper doily. Push
the flower stems through the central hole
in the doily and gather the doily around
the flowers.
Wrap aluminium foil around the kitchen
paper to keep the moisture in and conceal
the edge of the doily.
Tie ribbon in a bow.

Festive food

Simnel cake

Within the Dublin Pale the mistress of the house traditionally gave her maidservants the ingredients to make an iced fruitcake to take home to their mothers on Mothering Sunday.

Ingredients:
2 oz / 50g chopped blanched almonds
4 oz / 110g glacé cherries, cut into quarters
12 oz / 335g raisins
12 oz / 335g sultanas
12 oz / 335g currants
4 oz / 110g mixed chopped peel
2 oz / 50g ground almonds
Grated rind of one orange and one lemon
8 oz / 225g butter
1 fl oz whiskey or orange juice
8 oz / 225g soft brown sugar
6 eggs
10 oz / 275g plain white flour
1 large cooking apple
1 tsp mixed spice
2 lb / 900g marzipan

Method:
Preheat oven to gas 3 (160°C / 325°F).
Grease and line a round 9-inch (23cm) deep cake tin.
Mix the dried fruits, ground and chopped almonds, lemon and orange rind and leave to soak for 1 hour in the whiskey.
Cream the butter and sugar until light and fluffy. Beat in the eggs a little at a time. Stir in the spices and flour.
Add grated cooking apple to the fruit and then stir this into the cake mixture.
Put half of the cake mixture into the prepared tin.
Roll out half of the marzipan and place this on top and then cover with the rest of the cake mixture. Make a slight dip in the surface.
Bake for about 3 hours, lowering the temperature after the first hour.
Leave to stand in the tin overnight.
Next day, roll out the rest of the marzipan to cover the cake, saving a little to make into flowers, balls or other shapes to decorate the cake. Dust with icing sugar.

Palm Sunday

This is one week before Easter Sunday.

Church ceremonies commemorate Christ's entry into Jerusalem when the crowds waved palm branches and welcomed him with calls of Hosanna!

In Irish churches cypress, yew or pine branches served as the palm. People would take home from church a little sprig of the 'palm'.

Children start collecting eggs from neighbours from today for their Easter feast.

Things to make and do

Collect branches in bud that will open over the next week. Start collecting and blowing eggs to paint and hang from the Easter branch. (See Easter)

Easter grass

Sow grass or wheat seed in a basket filled with soil.
Water and watch as they sprout in time for Easter.

Sprout seeds for salad

You will need:
Alfalfa seeds, brown lentils or mung beans
Glass jar
Square of muslin

Method:
Place a thin layer of seeds in the bottom of the jar and pour in a little cold water. Swish it around then strain off the water.
Repeat, then cover the jar with a square of muslin held on by an elastic band.
Leave in a cool place out of direct sunlight.
Rinse and drain the seeds at least once a day, replacing the muslin cover each time. The seeds will begin to sprout within a few days. Alfalfa seeds are quicker to sprout than mung beans or lentils.
Eat them as a salad or include larger sprouts, particularly beansprouts, in a stir-fry.

Nest for eggs

You will need:
Straw, dried grass or hay
Moss, leaves and feathers
Darning needle and strong thread

Method:
Make a bundle of about twelve strands of
    grass, straw or hay.
Begin to coil the grasses to form a small mat,
    catching in place with the needle and
    thread.
Continue to coil the grasses, bringing the
    sides up gradually and stitching in place
    each few centimetres. Add more strands
    as needed.
Line the nest with moss, leaves or feathers
    until it looks soft and inviting. Leave it
    empty until Easter. If you leave the nest
    outside on Easter Sunday the Easter hare
    will drop an egg or two into it.

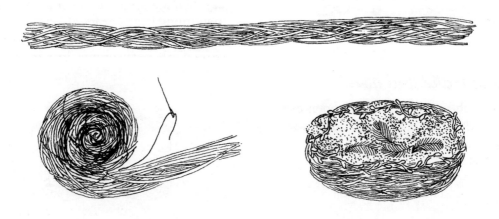

Easter

The word Easter has its root in *Oestrae,* an Anglo-Saxon version of Ostara, a Germanic goddess of light, spring and fertility. Easter is a moveable feast. Its date relates to both solar and lunar events and is calculated as the first Sunday after the full moon following the spring equinox. The timing of the Easter festival was one of the differences between the Celtic and the Roman churches in the sixth century.

In older times in Ireland, where possible, every member of the family would get new clothes at Easter. Children in particular would be given gifts of hats, shoes and stockings, which they would display proudly at church on Easter Sunday.

The egg, one of the major symbols of the Easter festival, is common to the creation stories of many cultures. It is easy to see why it is a symbol of resurrection. The hard shell must be pushed through and broken to reveal the golden sun within, with its promise of new life.

Good Friday

Good Friday was once a strict fast day, and there were many additional restrictions to be followed. No work that involved cutting wood or driving in nails was done, no animals were slaughtered and no fishing undertaken.

However it was considered a good time to give the house and yard a thorough cleaning and tidying. Sowing a little seed corn or a few potatoes on Good Friday was thought to bring a blessing onto the whole crop.

Eggs laid today are marked with a cross and kept for eating on Easter Sunday. Any eggs hatched on Good Friday would grow to be healthy birds. All bread baked on Good Friday should be marked with a cross.

Water from holy wells has special curative powers on Good Friday, so people often visit wells and take home a little of the water as a cure for illnesses. Others visit family graves and pray for the souls of departed relatives.

A child born on Good Friday and baptised on Easter Sunday is destined to be a healer, while anyone who dies on this day is meant to go straight to heaven.

Most people went to church on Good Friday and silence was encouraged between noon and 3 p.m., the time when Christ was upon the cross. In Celtic Christianity, Christ was believed to be King of the Elements and the elements were thought to respond to his death. The sky was expected to darken; and cold, wet weather was taken as a sign of nature's mourning.

On Easter Saturday people would take three sips of blessed water as a preventive against illness for the coming year.

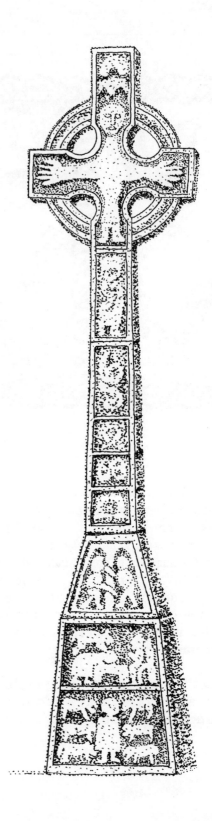

Hot Cross Buns

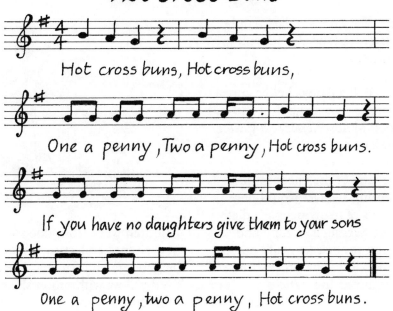

Hot cross buns, Hot cross buns,

One a penny, Two a penny, Hot cross buns.

If you have no daughters give them to your sons

One a penny, two a penny, Hot cross buns.

Hot Cross Buns

Hot Cross Buns, Hot Cross Buns,
One a penny, two a penny,
Hot Cross Buns.
If you have no daughters,
Give them to your sons
One a penny, two a penny
Hot Cross Buns

Festive food

Hot Cross Buns

Ingredients:
1/2 pint / 275ml milk
Dried yeast
6 oz / 160g mixed dried fruit and peel
1 tsp mixed spice
Pinch salt
2 oz / 50g sugar
1 lb / 450g strong white flour
3 oz / 75g butter
2 beaten eggs

Method:
Warm the milk to body temperature and add
the dried yeast, butter and a teaspoon of
brown sugar. Stir and leave to sit for a
moment. Mix in the eggs and sugar.
Sift the flour and spices into a large bowl.
Make a well in the centre and pour in the
liquids. Mix together with a wooden
spoon, adding more milk if necessary.
Turn out onto a floured surface and press in
the dried fruit. Knead the dough and then
return to the bowl and cover with a clean
tea towel. Leave it in a warm place until
doubled in size.
Knead the dough for a few minutes and then
shape into buns. Place these on a greased
baking sheet and leave to rise again.
Make a small quantity of shortcrust pastry.
Roll out the pastry and cut into thin strips.
Brush the tops of the buns with a glaze made
of milk with a little sugar dissolved in it.
Lay the pastry strips on the buns to form
crosses.
Bake at gas mark 7 (220°C / 425°F) for 15
minutes. Cool on a wire rack.

Easter Sunday

On the morning of Easter Sunday people climb hills to watch the sun dance with joy for the risen Christ.

In many towns butchers' boys held a mock funeral for a herring, as a symbol of the end of the long period of abstinence, on Easter Sunday or Monday.

The herring was one of the cheapest fish available and, during Lent, it would have been the main part of many people's diet. The boys tied the herring to a rope and dragged it through the streets while others beat the fish with sticks. The procession was accompanied by music and dancing.

There are many customs concerning eggs on Easter Sunday, of course. The egg has always been a potent symbol of regeneration and renewal. Eggs were not eaten during Lent so there would be a bountiful supply of them available for feasting and games.

Eggs are eaten for breakfast, they are given as gifts and hidden and hunted; and are also painted and decorated. There is a saying that, 'Nobody should be without an egg at Easter.' People often gave gifts of their surplus eggs to the poor and needy.

Children went from door to door in their new clothes collecting gifts of eggs from neighbours and friends. The eggs were often dyed yellow with onion skins. The children took their bounty, along with a picnic of bread and cake, to a quiet spot to cook outside, away from the adults. This was known as a *clúdóg*.

They also made simple spoons to eat their eggs with out of scraps of wood. Broken eggshells, particularly those that had been coloured, were kept to decorate the May Bush. (See Bealtaine)

Egg rolling is a custom among the Ulster Scots in the North of Ireland. Children paint or colour hard-boiled eggs and take them up a slope to roll them downhill. Whoever cracks an opponent's egg, can claim and eat it. This is done in memory of the stone being rolled away from the tomb on the first Easter Sunday.

A 'cake dance' was held on the evening of Easter Sunday in most parishes. All the courting couples of the area would come to the dance. This was a dance held outdoors, often at a crossroads, with a large cake as a prize for the finest dancers. The cake was displayed on a white cloth spread on an upturned churndash, surrounded by flowers and ribbons. The best dancing couple took down the cake and divided it among the other dancers. This is probably the origin of the saying 'That takes the cake'.

Holy wells were visited and their waters taken as a cure on Easter Sunday. It was also a fine day for walking in the countryside, visiting standing stones and decorating them with flowers.

The dancing hare

A friend told me a story of something that happened on Easter morning when her daughter Triona was four years old.

The family was renovating an old house in rural County Clare. When they opened the curtains that morning they saw a thick mist covering the fields, stretching away before them like a great sea.

Opening the house door to take in the fresh morning air, they breathed in the beauty of sun and mist, light and mystery. Triona noticed something moving in the mist, and called her mother to watch. As they sat, silently, they saw that it was a hare.

They watched as he spun and turned this way and that, until at last he leapt out through the dyke and away. With absolute certainty Triona whispered, 'The Easter hare'.

The Cock that Crowed

*H*AVE *you ever wondered what it is the cockerel says when he crows? There is an old tale that explains it all.*

Long ago, when Christ's body was laid in the tomb, the people talked about his supporters' claim that he would rise again on the third day.

People said, 'Probably his followers will steal away his body and claim that he has risen.'

'There will be trouble then. We must prevent them from entering the tomb.'

The leader of the people said, 'I know. We must place a mighty boulder before the mouth of the cave. Then no one can enter – and no one leave the tomb.' So several strong men were hired to close the tomb's mouth with a flagstone. They sweated and puffed, so great was the stone, but at last they heaved it into place. The tomb was sealed. When it was done, a feast was held. Among the delicacies for the feast, a pot of cockerels boiled over a fire.

When the labourers had washed and came to join the feast, the leader asked, 'Is it well done? Is the cave mouth sealed?' 'Aye, it is done,' the labourers answered. 'No man can rise out of that cave now, no more than the cockerel in that pot can rise from the dead!' The others threw back their heads to laugh, but stopped short, aghast. One of the cockerels rose up out of the broth in the pot, flapping his wings and throwing back his head to call, 'Mary's son is risen!' So, whenever the cockerel crows at Easter time, he reminds us that Mary's son rose from the tomb.

A Sign in the Sky

CONCHOBAR MAC NESSA was the son of Nessa, a queen, and Cathbad, a druid. Before he was born, a prophecy foretold that a great king would be born on a certain day. And so when Conchobar was born, far away in another land, at that same moment, Jesus Christ was born. Conchobar grew to become King of Ulster.

When King Conchobar defeated Meisceadhra in battle he made a trophy of his enemy's brain by mixing it with lime, leaving it to dry till it formed a small hard ball. He held the brainball high for all to see at the feast that night, boasting of his prowess in the contest. Within the hall whispers spread the tale of a prophecy that Meisceadhra's brain would avenge itself after his death. And so it came to be.

An enemy of the king stole the trophy. Now, in those unruly days hurling was just as popular a sport as it is today, though perhaps a rougher game was played. One day, in a game, this man hurled the brainball at Conchobar so hard that it lodged deeply in the king's skull.

The druid healer came to tend the injured king. He bound the wound in Conchobar's head with a golden band that matched the colour of his hair. However, the ball could not be removed, so deeply embedded was it within his own brain that to extract it might kill the king. The wound healed over, Conchobar recovered well, richly rewarded his physician and went on with his kingly business.

Seven years later, Conchobar stood on a hilltop with his druid, watching a strange phenomenon in the sky. The sun was eclipsed, the sky grew dark and the moon shone full during the day. Conchobar, witnessing this wonder, spoke with his druid, asking 'What manner of thing is this? It is as if the elements themselves revolt! What is it makes this change in the heavens and on the earth?'

The druid answered him, 'At this moment, in another land, God's son hangs upon a cross. His death draws near and nature mourns his passing.'

'It is a great pity that such a noble man is crucified,' said Conchobar. 'If I were there I would take up my sword and slay those who put him to his death.' And in his rage he threw off his cloak and drew his sword. Then battle frenzy overtook his senses and he raced down the hill towards a great oak wood, thinking the trees to be a mighty army. As he slashed and cut and turned and hewed, tree after mighty tree fell around him, until he raised his sword once more and fell himself. So great was his fury on behalf of Mary's Son that his old wound tore open and the brainball shot out of his head. This time the wound could not be sealed and Conchobar died of his exertions on this most memorable of days.

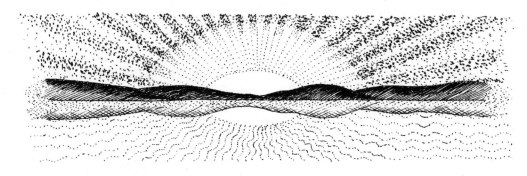

Things to make and do

Watch the sun dance

Climb a hill and watch the sunrise from a high place. Bear in mind that it is not a good idea for children to look directly at the sun. However they can watch its reflection in a bucket or tub of water, or on the surface of a well or a lake. You could also place a bowl of water on the inside windowsill so that the sun's reflection can be seen dancing on the walls and ceiling of your house.

Visit a holy well

See Lughnasadh.

Clúdóg

You will need:
Newspaper and kindling
Small sticks
Old saucepan
Uncooked eggs
Teacups
Butter

Method:
Clúdóg is a name used for a collection of eggs, the picnic feast where the eggs are cooked, and also for the little play house made for the picnic.
Collect uncooked eggs from friends and family. Take these in an old sock and look for a suitable place in the garden to build a den.

Get an adult to build a small fire and cook the eggs in the saucepan over the fire.
Eat them outside with butter in a cup using a rough and ready spoon.

Rough and ready egg spoon

You will need:
Penknife
Small twig

Method:
Remove the bark from the twig and whittle away until the twig has a flat surface on top. Do the same on the other side.
Shave away at one end to form a narrow handle, leaving the spoon end wider, like a flat paddle.

Egg hunt

The Easter hare often brings little chocolate eggs on Easter morning, but you will have to go out and look for them. They may not be where you would expect!

A small rush basket that will hold one or two little chocolate eggs can be made quite simply. See **Fairy basket** in the Lughnasadh section.

Onion-dyed eggs

You will need:
Uncooked eggs
Onion skins
Small leaves or paper shapes
Vinegar
Old nylon tights cut into 15cm / 6 inch
   lengths
Thread or string
Old pan

Method:
Wash the egg and leave it wet. Carefully
   place a leaf on the egg, smoothing it out
   (figure 1).
Wrap onion skins around the egg until it is
   well covered (figure 2).
Wrap a length of nylon tights around the
   egg. Pull it tightly so that it will hold
   everything in place and fasten with thread
   (figure 3).
Fill a saucepan with enough water to cover
   your eggs. Add the eggs and a teaspoon of
   vinegar. Bring to the boil, and boil for 10
   minutes. Remove the eggs and cool them
   under the tap.
Unwrap the eggs and you will find a leaf
   pattern. You can polish your eggs with a
   little sunflower oil.
You can also dye eggs with gorse flowers for
a yellow, or beetroot for a pinkish-red
colour.
You can follow this same procedure using
   Easter shapes cut out of paper instead of
   the leaves. You could use, for example, a
   hare, chick, flower or butterfly.

Egg rolling

Take your boiled eggs for a walk up a hill.
Roll the eggs down the hill. Whose egg
reaches the bottom first? Whose egg gets
there without being cracked? Once an egg is
cracked open, you can eat it.

Blowing eggs

You will need:
Eggs
Large needle

Method:
Wash the egg thoroughly.
Use the needle to make two holes in the
   shell, a small one at the top and a bigger
   one at the bottom.
Pierce the egg yolk inside with the needle.
   Holding the egg over a bowl, blow into
   the smaller hole. The white and yolk will
   run out the larger hole into the bowl.
Wash the egg again in soapy water with a
   little vinegar added. Allow it to dry.

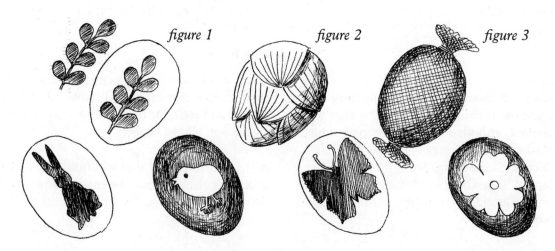

figure 1   *figure 2*   *figure 3*

Painting blown eggs

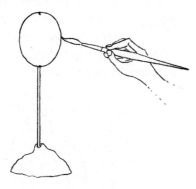

You will need:
Newspaper
Paints
Fine paintbrushes
Water
Knitting needle and plasticine

Method:
Put the egg onto the knitting needle and
stick this into some plasticine. This will
hold the egg while you paint it. Paint the
egg as you wish. You can cover it in a
single colour or paint patterns on it.
You can also draw a design on the egg with a
white wax crayon and then paint over this.
This will leave the waxed areas free of
paint.

To hang the egg

You will need:
Long needle
Thread
Matchstick

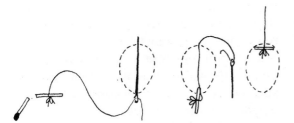

Method:
Break the match in half. Tie a thread half
way along the piece of matchstick.
Use the needle to draw the thread through
the large hole in the egg and out through
the small hole.
Push the match inside the egg. This will hold
the thread in place. Tie a loop at the other
end to hang the egg on your Easter branch.

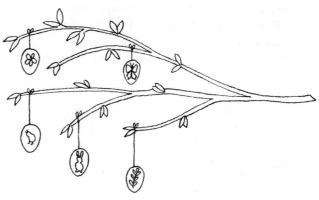

Woven paper basket

You will need:
Thick handmade paper in two colours, e.g.
yellow and cream
Thin cream card
Scissors or craft knife
Stapler
Glue
Clothes pegs

Method:

Cut nine strips of cream paper 2cm wide by 32cm long / ³/4 x 12¹/2 inches.

Place five strips together in a row, as shown in figure 1.

figure 1

Take four more strips and weave these through at right angles, leaving equal lengths at both ends (figure 2).

Staple the corners to hold this 'mat' in place (figure 3).

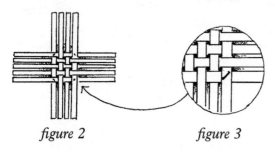

figure 2   *figure 3*

Bend the strips up to form the uprights for weaving the sides of the basket. Cut four strips of yellow paper, 2 x 43cm / ³/4 x 17 inches.

Weave these strips in and out of the uprights, one strip at a time. Glue in place at beginning and end of each strip.

When you have finished the weaving, stick each of the cream uprights to the last yellow weaver with glue and hold in place with clothes pegs (figure 4).

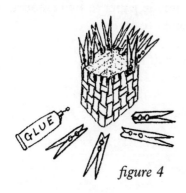

figure 4

Trim off the excess of the cream strips once the glue is dry. Cut a strip from the cream paper 4 x 40cm / 1¹/2 x 16 inches.

Fold in half lengthways and glue over the top edge of the basket (figure 5). Hold in place with clothes pegs.

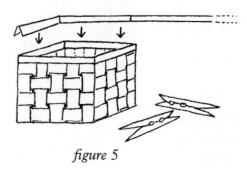

figure 5

Cut a strip of cream card 3 x 28cm / 1 x 11 inches) for a handle.

Glue 3cm / 1 inch at each end to the basket and hold in place with clothes pegs until dry.

Line with straw or shredded paper and a few small eggs.

Mother hen and her chicks

You will need:
Yellow or cream wool for chicks
Brown wool for mother hen
3mm knitting needles
Scraps of orange and red felt

Method:

For the chicks:
Cast on 20 stitches. Knit 3 rows in garter stitch (plain).

At the beginning of each of the following rows knit two together.

Continue until only four stitches remain. Draw a thread through these four stitches and sew up the diagonal sides (see diagram on the next page).

Fill the chick with fleece or cotton wool and sew up the bottom.

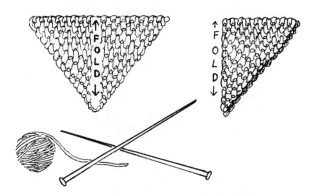

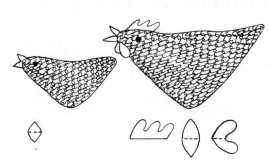

Give the chick a beak made from a scrap of orange felt and sew two eyes with a dark thread.

For the mother hen:

Follow the same pattern as above, beginning with 30 stitches.

When the hen has been sewn up, cut a comb, beak and gills from red felt and sew these on. Sew eyes with a thick dark thread.

For those who cannot knit, a triangle of yellow or brown felt can be sewn as above to form the chick or hen.

An Easter border

You will need:

Thin yellow paper
Scissors
Pencil
Ruler

Method:

Cut a strip of paper 6.5cm / 2½ inches wide and about 25cm / 10 inches long.

Measure 5cm / 2 inches from the beginning on the long edge and mark this point. Fold the paper backwards at the mark.

Fold again after another 5cm / 2 inches and so on until the whole paper is folded like a concertina, being careful that the folds are straight and accurate.

Copy the egg and chick from the diagram onto the paper, making sure that the dotted lines sit on the folds.

Cut out along the solid lines. Be careful not to cut along the folds. Unfold to reveal a line of chicks and eggs.

You can use a longer strip of paper or join several together to make a longer frieze.

April Fool's Day, 1 April

In older times it was common on April Fool's Day for a foolish young person to be sent a few miles with a letter for a neighbour.

When the letter was handed over the recipient read the message, 'Send the fool further.' So, he would hand the letter back to the 'fool' and direct him to take it to the next village for someone there.

The next recipient would read the same message and again send the 'fool' another mile or so. And so it would go on until someone took pity on the poor fool.

Nowadays it is a time for playing practical jokes – but only up till 12 noon. Anyone who tries to play an April Fool trick after noon is called a fool himself!

April Fool

A duck in the pond, a fish in the pool,
Whoever reads this is a big April fool!

But April Fool is past and gone
And you're the fool to carry it on.

A duck in the pond a fish in the pool, whoever reads this is a big April fool.

Weather lore

Thunder in April, Floods in May. A cold April and a full barn.

When April blows its horn 'tis good for hay and corn.

Summer months

Bealtaine

Bealtaine, 1 May

(pronounced Bee-all-tenn-a) *Also known as May Day.*

The first of May is the beginning of summer. This is the light half of the year, when the sun grows to its height at midsummer and then begins to wane until, at Samhain, the dark half of the year begins again. The sun grows stronger and this is celebrated with fires and dancing.

In the agricultural year, Bealtaine was the time when cattle were moved to the *buaile* or high summer pastures. All seed crops had already been planted by this time and growth was underway. It was also the time when turf cutting for the winter's supply of fuel began. Land rental and work contracts were renewed on the first of May and hiring fairs were held.

Farmers walked the perimeter of their lands after sunset on Bealtaine Eve, stopping to acknowledge the four directions, beginning with the east, then south, west and north.

They would drop a little seed and water from a holy well, or some ash from the Bealtaine fire in each quarter. This was also done within the house, lighting a candle and blessing the threshold, the hearth, the four corners and then the inhabitants.

The Bealtaine fire

Bealtaine fires were lit as beacons on hilltops. The first fire was lit on the hill of Uisneach at the centre of Ireland. When the Uisneach fire was seen from afar, this was a signal to light the fire on the local hill and so the fires spread, radiating out from there until a network of hilltop fires was alight throughout the country, re-enlivening the land with the warmth of the sun. In every home, the fire was put out and rekindled from a spark from the sacred fire. The Bealtaine bonfire is still lit in Limerick City.

Farmers singed the tails of their cattle with an ember from the fire or drove their cattle between two bonfires as a purification. Just ten years ago I saw a farmer in Co Clare driving his cattle between the fires on May Eve.

The fairies at Bealtaine

Just as the cattle are moved from the winter to summer pastures, so too the Good People, the fairies, move from their winter residence to their summer palaces. They are therefore very active at this time and are often on the look out for healthy babies to snatch, and nursing mothers to tend the stolen children.

Precautions include carrying a piece of iron such as a pin, or best of all, a black-handled knife. To look through a sprig of rowan twisted into a ring enables one to see the fairies. The fairies were often honoured by leaving a gift of food or drink on the threshold or at a fairy thorn or mound.

A child born on May Day would be able to see the fairies.

Butter could easily be stolen by a neighbour using a magical charm on May Day, as could the fertility of one's fields or cattle, so every precaution was taken to prevent this. No coal was taken from the fire because someone could use this to charm the butter away. Nothing was loaned or given as a gift 'no spending, no lending, no borrowing' was the rule on May Day.

The May bush

The summer was welcomed by setting up a May bush. Flowers, mostly yellow flowers as these are most plentiful at this time – furze (gorse), buttercups, celandine, primroses, marigolds, cowslips – were gathered before dusk on May Eve. These were made into posies and hung over windows and doors or strewn loose on the threshold and floor of the house. They might also be tied to cows' horns or tails or to agricultural equipment. Children brought flowers to the old and lonely of the community.

Weather lore

A wet and windy May fill the barns with corn and hay

A wet May and dry June make the farmer whistle a tune

A swarm of bees in May is worth a load of hay

The May bush – a branch or bough of a tree – was set up outside the house in the yard or fields to guard against bad luck. Whitethorn was the most popular tree for the May bush. In different parts of the country different trees were used, some places favouring the sycamore, others rowan, hazel or elder. The May bush was decorated with flowers, ribbons, streamers and coloured eggshells saved from Easter eggs. In Dublin children collected contributions for decorating the May bush, saying 'Long life, a pretty wife and a candle for the May bush.'

May games

May poles were not so common as bushes, but appeared in Ulster and in towns and cities in Leinster where English influence was strong. A tall straight tree was smoothed off, set up and decorated. People danced in a circle around the pole. Another custom was to smear the pole with grease and hold a contest with a prize for the one that could climb to the top. Other sports included races on foot, sack races, blindfold chases, grinning through horse collars, wrestling, hopping and jumping contests.

Processions

In Ulster, May boys in white shirts bedecked with ribbons marched in a procession led by a May queen and king. In other places bands of young men and women dressed in white and decorated with ribbons on their hats, shoulders and shirt sleeves, carried a bush containing two hurling balls – one gold and one silver. A band of musicians led the procession and a 'fool' and a 'female fool' walked alongside, splashing water on the crowds. A 'May baby' made of flowers was carried by some processions and an old custom says that childless women who touch the May baby will conceive.

The Piper Who Knew But One Tune

*L*ONG AGO *there lived a young piper in county Galway. He was known as a foolish boy, with only half his wits, and he lived with his mother in a little cabin. Though he dearly loved the music, he could play but the one tune over and over. The rich folks of the parish thought it great sport to pay the fool to play for their amusement. And so on May Eve he was walking home from a dance in one of the big houses. Just as he stepped onto the little bridge over the stream, a fine figure on a silver pony stopped him in his tracks, raising his hand and calling, 'Piper, play for me the Shan Van Vocht.'*

'Right gladly I'd play it for you sir, but I don't know it at all,' said the piper. 'I only have the one tune I can play and it's not the Shan Van Vocht.'

'Pick up your pipes and I'll make you know it,' commanded the fairy man.

So the piper filled his bag with wind and began to play his old familiar tune. But as he played new strains came through until the music broke into the Shan Van Vocht, then Sí Beag Sí Mor and many other tunes that he had never played before. The piper began to dance as he played, crying, 'My, but you're a fine teacher!'

'Now that you can play,' said the fairy man, 'you must come with me. There is a celebration tonight at the house of the Fairy Queen. A piper is needed to play for the dancing and you will be well rewarded for your troubles.'

So up on the back of the silver pony behind the fairy man climbed the piper. Through the fields and over the mountains they seemed to fly at great speed till at last they came to rest high on a bleak mountainside. Before the piper had time for second thoughts, the fairy man tapped three times with his heel on a great stone in the side of the mountain. A door opened into a hall brightly lit by candles and lamps. At a long golden table laid with a fine damask cloth, sat hundreds of fairy folk, dressed in silks, brocades and velvets. Before them were dishes of silver piled high with sweetmeats and delicacies and in their hands goblets of crystal. These they raised in a toast, calling, 'The piper has arrived!'

The Fairy Queen beckoned him towards her, saying, 'A hundred thousand welcomes to the finest piper in the land.'

When she clicked her fingers, three serving boys brought a fine embroidered suit, with a waistcoat and all, and helped the piper change his clothes so that he looked as bright and merry as the assembled host. At last she called, 'Let the dancing begin!'

And so the piper who knew but one tune took up his pipes and began to play. One tune ran on into the next without a break to catch the breath, and so bright and joyful was the music that the fairy host danced the whole night through, the hall ringing and shaking with their merriment.

At last the Fairy Queen called, 'Enough,' and stepped forward to pay the piper. Into his hat she dropped gold pieces. Each of the dancers dropped in a piece of gold till his hat was stretched out of shape with the weight of them.

'Come now,' said the fairy man, 'and I'll bring you home again.'

Back over the hills they flew till the piper's familiar fields came into view. The fairy man set him down on the little bridge, saying, 'Go home now piper and take with you two things you never had before – good sense and the gift of music. May you use them well. Farewell.'

The piper walked on to his mother's cabin. He knocked on the door calling, 'Open the door Mammy to the finest piper in all Ireland!'

'Quiet, my poor fool of a boy. Come away in now.'

He emptied the gold coins from his hat into his mother's apron and he strapped on his pipes.

'Listen Mammy, till you hear what music I can play.'

As he squeezed the bag, the first sound came out like a frightened goose. His mother shook her head at her foolish son's delusions, and turned sadly away. But before she had left the room, she turned back and began to dance as out of the pipes came the most melodious of music, all the tunes of the fairy host and more besides. Soon the neighbours came and the folks from the next village till the meadows were filled with music and dancing.

And from that day forth until the day he died, the piper was known as the finest in the county Galway, if not in all Ireland.

The Fairies (A Child's Song)

Up the airy mountain
Down the rushy glen,
We daren't go a-hunting,
For fear of little men;
Wee folk, good folk,
Trooping all together;
Green jacket, red cap,
And white owl's feather.

Down along the rocky shore
Some make their home,
They live on crispy pancakes
Of yellow tide-foam;
Some in the reeds
Of the black mountain-lake,
With frogs for their watch-dogs,
All night awake.

High on the hill-top
The old King sits;
He is now so old and gray
He's nigh lost his wits.
With a bridge of white mist
Columbkill he crosses,
On his stately journeys
From Slieveleague to Rosses;
Or going up with music,
On cold starry nights,
To sup with the Queen,
Of the gay Northern Lights.

They stole little Bridget
For seven years long;
When she came down again
Her friends were all gone.
They took her lightly back
Between the night and morrow;
They thought she was fast asleep,
But she was dead with sorrow.
They have kept her ever since
Deep within the lake,
On a bed of flag leaves,
Watching till she wake.

By the craggy hill-side,
Through the mosses bare,
They have planted thorn trees
For pleasure here and there.
Is any man so daring
As dig them up in spite?
He shall find the thornies set
In his bed at night.

Up the airy mountain
Down the rushy glen,
We daren't go a-hunting,
For fear of little men;
Wee folk, good folk,
Trooping all together;
Green jacket, red cap,
And white owl's feather.

William Allingham (1824 – 1889)

Things to make

May bush

You will need:
Branches with leaves and buds or blossom
Large plant pot filled with stones and earth
   or a small tree in a pot
Coloured ribbons
Paper streamers
Stars, flowers, silver and gold balls, painted
   eggshells
White shirt or dress

Method:
Arrange the branch in the plant pot so that it
   is stable and firm.
Decorate the branch with coloured ribbons,
   streamers, hanging eggshells and balls.
Place the May bush in the garden and dance
   or play circle games around it, wearing a
   white shirt or dress to which you have
   sewn ribbons and a floral crown.

Simple flower garland

You will need:
Lots of flowers
Needle and thread

Method:
Thread the needle with a doubled thread and tie a large knot at the end. Push the needle through the first flower and push the flower down to the knot at the end of the thread.

Continue to thread flowers in a spiral, as if stringing a necklace with beads. The thread will be concealed in the middle of the flowers.

You can use different coloured flowers and add in small leaves now and then for variation. Bluebells, horse chestnut flowers, lilac, daisies and many other wild or garden flowers can be strung in this way.

Flower garland 2

You will need:
Flowers with short stems
Strong thread

Method:
Cut two lengths of thread each about twice the length of the finished garland.

Cut another thread four times the length of the finished garland. Tie the three strands together at one end.

Hold the threads by the knotted end with the single long thread to the left. Insert the sepal of the first flower between the two shorter threads.

Bring the single thread round in front of the flower, over the pair of short threads, around behind them and back over the long thread as shown in the diagram.

Pull the thread to tighten it and repeat to make a double knot that will hold the flower in place.

Insert another flower, push it up against the knot and tie it into place. Continue until you reach the end of the thread.

If the garland is too small, simply tie on more thread and continue in the same way.

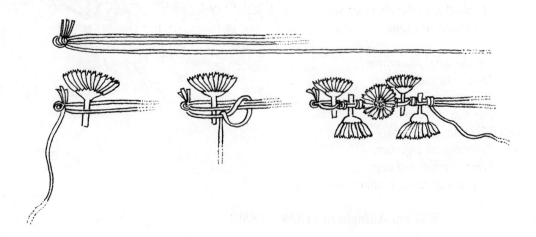

Floral crown

You will need:
Straw or hay
Flowers and leaves
Twine or florists wire
Thread

Method:
Take a bundle of straw and bind into a
crown with twine, adding more or pulling
out stalks to make the right length to fit
around your head.

Form it into a circle, overlapping the ends,
and bind it with twine or wire.

Gather flowers and leaves (you can use dried
flowers if you don't have any fresh flowers
available).

Cover the straw with leaves, poking their
stalks into the straw and tying in place
with twine.

Make little bunches of flowers and tie
together with thread. Add flower bunches
to the crown, laying in place and then
binding with twine, arranging so that the
leaves cover the wires.

A May ball

The May ball was a decorated hurling ball
which would be used in a game after the
procession. Here are instructions for a
portable beach ball that can be blown up
and played with time and time again. The
outside is made of cloth and inside is a
balloon, so that if the ball bursts, you only
have to replace the balloon.

You will need:
Strong round balloon
Brightly coloured heavy cotton fabric
Scissors
Needle and thread

Method:
Copy onto paper the pattern on the next
page. Pin to your fabric and cut out three
hexagonal pieces (A) and six of piece B.

With right sides facing each other, pin each
B piece to one of the hexagons, as shown
and sew.

With right sides facing in, pin and sew up
the long sides. Leave a gap of about 5cm /
2 inches on one of the sides, to allow the
ball to be turned right sides out.

Place two hexagons together right sides out,
and sew around the edges to hold them
together.

Cut a slit and make a buttonhole about 2cm
/ 1 inch long. To make the buttonhole,
you will need to sew small blanket stitches
close together, along the cut edge of the
slit. This prevents the fabric from fraying.

Sew the other short sides to this hexagon.
The entire ball is now outside in.

Turn the ball the right way out by pushing it
through the gap in one of the sides. Close
the gap with a few stitches.

Push a strong balloon in through the buttonhole and blow it up to fill the fabric ball.

Tie a knot and push the knot inside the ball.

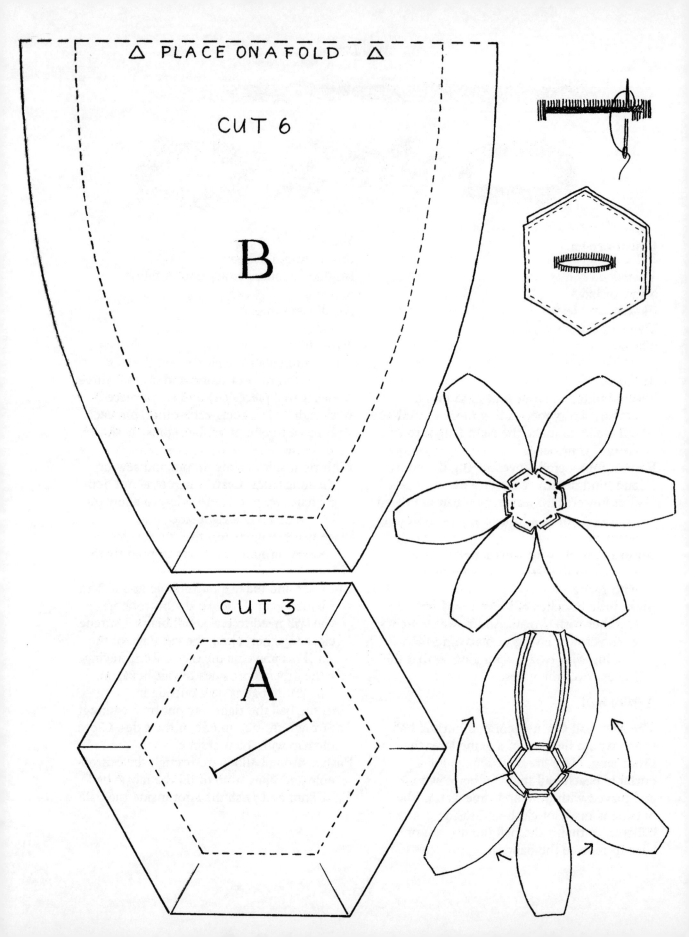

PLACE ON A FOLD

CUT 6

B

CUT 3

A

Games

On May Day ... all the young
men and women hold hands
and dance in a circle ...
moving in curves from right to
left as if imitating the windings
of a serpent.

*Wilde's Ancient Cures, Charms
and Usages of Ireland*

Dusky Bluebells

In and out the dusky bluebells, In and out the dusky bluebells

In and out the dusky bluebells, I am the master.

In and out the dusky bluebells

In and out the dusky bluebells,
In and out the dusky bluebells,
In and out the dusky bluebells,
I'll be your master.

Tipper ripper rapper on your shoulder,
Tipper ripper rapper on your shoulder,
Tipper ripper rapper on your shoulder,
I'll be your master.

Children stand in a circle holding hands.
They raise their hands in the air to form
arches.

One player is chosen as 'the master' and
weaves in and out of the arches moving to
the left around the circle while the others
sing the first verse.

At the end of verse one, the master stops
behind one of the children in the circle
and taps on her shoulders while the group
sings the second verse.

This child then leaves the circle and holding
onto the waist of the master follows her as
she begins again to weave through the
circle of arches while the group sings
verse one again.

This continues until there are no arches left
to pass through.

Nuts in May

Nuts, of course, do not grow in May. It is possible that the original song had a mis-spelling of an old Anglo-Irish word 'knots', which meant posies or bunches of blossom.

These knots would have been used to decorate the house and the May bush.

Here we come gathering nuts in May, nuts in May, nuts in May.
Here we come gathering nuts in May, Ear-ly in the morning.

Here we come gathering nuts in May
Nuts in May, nuts in May
Here we come gathering nuts in May
Early in the morning.

Who will you choose for nuts in May
Nuts in May, nuts in May
Who will you choose for nuts in May early in
the morning?

(Eileen Brady) for nuts in May
Nuts in May, nuts in May
(Eileen Brady) for nuts in May early in the
morning.

Very well and so you may
So you may, so you may,
Very well and so you may, early in the morning.

Who will you choose to take her away
Take her away, take her away,
Who will you choose to take her away early in
the morning?

(Aidan Walsh) to take her away
Take her away, take her away
(Aidan Walsh) to take her away early in the
morning.

Players face each other in two lines, A and B, with space between to walk forwards and backwards as they sing alternate verses of the song.

The song is a question and answer. Line A sings the first verse, line B sings the second, and so on.

After the last verse, the two named children face each other over a central mark (e.g. a chalk mark or a stone on the ground). Each tries to pull the other over the mark.

The child that is pulled over joins the other side as a captured 'nut'. So the game begins again.

Ball games

Many games can be played with a small rubber ball, bouncing it on the ground or against a wall. Rhymes are used to keep count as the ball is bounced or thrown.

Mary Mac, Mac, Mac
Dressed in black, black, black
Silver buttons, buttons, buttons
Down her back, back, back.

One two three O'Leary
Four five six O'Leary
Seven eight nine O'Leary
Ten O'Leary Postman

Queenie, queenie Caroline
Washed her hair in turpentine
Turpentine makes it shine
Queenie, queenie Caroline.

To make the game a little more complicated, actions, such as pointing one toe or another, spinning around, touching the ground, clapping hands can be introduced between throws.

I've a bike, a fairy bike

I only got it Friday night

I went up the hill (throw ball against the wall and let it bounce once on the ground before catching)

Down the hill (bounce ball once on the ground before it hits the wall)

Under the arch (throw ball from behind so it goes through the legs and bounces on the ground before hitting the wall)

And a rainbow. (draw a rainbow in the air with your hand while the ball is still in the air)

Races and sports

Sack race

You will need:
One sack per player
Whistle
Hessian sacks are best, but coal sacks or fertiliser bags are easier to find these days

How to play:
Mark a starting line and a finishing line on the ground. All contestants line up at the starting place with their legs inside a sack.

The starter blows the whistle as the signal that the contest begins. The players jump in their sacks as fast as they can towards the finishing line.

The winner is the first over the line.

Three-legged race

You will need:
An even number of players

How to play:
Each player is given a partner. It is probably best if adults and children are mixed together fairly.

Partners are tied together in this way: partner A's left ankle is tied to partner B's right ankle. This way, they have three legs between them.

Contestants line up at the starting line and wait for the whistle. Winners are the first couple over the finishing line.

Grinning or gurning

Grinning was one of the contests at the May Day gatherings. This was played using an old horse collar. Each player put his head through the collar and pulled a grotesque face. A prize was given to the most gifted grinner.

You may not have a horse collar – instead you could use a picture frame, toilet seat or a cardboard box with a square cut out of one side, which might then resemble a television set. This can be placed on the player's head,

leaving hands free to help pull a face. Players take it in turn to place their heads through the horse collar and pull a face. The more distorted and grotesque the better!

Things to do

May dew for health and beauty

The dew on May morning also has special properties. Girls still rise at dawn to wash their faces in the May Dew to ensure a fine complexion.

To gather May dew: rise before dawn and gather the dew on a linen cloth, wring it out into a dish and pour it into a bottle. Keep the jar in full sunlight for a few days and then any pour off any sediment. This was known as a cure for sunburn, freckles, headaches, skin complaints and sore eyes.

A man who washed his hands in May dew could untie any knot and open any lock. The first water drawn from the well on May Day also had healing powers.

Gathering herbs

May Day was a good time to pick medicinal herbs. It is said that any herb picked at random before sunrise on May Day would be a cure for warts. To eat a meal of nettles three days in a row was a good tonic.

Pick herbs on a sunny morning after the dew has dried. Between 10 a.m. and noon is probably the best time. It is traditional to pick flowers, berries and leaves at the full moon, and roots at the new moon.

Be careful where you gather your herbs. Don't pick from the sides of busy roads. You can use scissors or just your fingertips to gather the herbs. Place them in a wicker basket. It is best to ask permission before picking and to leave a gift for the fairies (e.g., you might sprinkle some lavender flowers on the ground, bury a silver coin in the earth, or whatever seems appropriate).

Process the herbs as soon as possible after harvesting. Don't leave them lying around, as they will quickly lose their vitality.

Washing delicate flowers will bruise them, so instead pick with care and remove any insects or debris by hand. If you plan to make an oil infusion, again don't wash your herbs.

Drying herbs

Hang them in loose bunches or lay them out on a cloth on a tray. Keep out of sunlight in a warm place with good ventilation. A hot press (airing cupboard) is a good place to dry herbs. Most herbs dry quickly, within a few days.

Comfrey Poultice

For bumps, bruises, sprains, bone, ligaments and cartilage injuries

Use the large fresh leaves of comfrey. Put 6 leaves in a pan with a little bit of cider vinegar. Soften the leaves over a gentle heat, without cooking.
Remove the leaves and roll them out flat between two layers of muslin.
Put a little vegetable oil on the skin of the affected part and then wrap the poultice around and bandage it on.

Riddle

I wash my face in water that has never rained nor run,
and dry it on a towel that was neither wove nor spun.

(Washed in the May dew and dried in the open air)

Turf modelling

Turf (or peat as it is known elsewhere) is a traditional fuel in Ireland. Large areas of the country are covered in peat bogs. At one time each small farmer would have had turbery rights – the right to cut turf in a local bog for the year's fuel supply.

Turf is cut with a special spade called a *slán*. It is footed or left to dry in little pyramid-shaped piles. Later it is stacked into a large heap or brought home to fill a shed. Moist freshly cut turf can be squeezed like clay and formed into little animals. As the turf slowly dries out the model will shrink and harden.

May Day divination

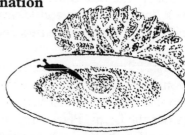

You will need:
A slug
Cabbage leaf
Flour
Plate

Method:
On May morning, before the sun has risen, go to the garden and find a small slug.
Put the slug on a plate dusted with flour and cover the plate with a large cabbage leaf.
Leave it covered until after the sunrise. The slug's trail in the flour will define your true love's initials.

The Short Cut to Rosses

By the short cut to Rosses a fairy girl I met;
I was taken in her beauty as a fish is in a net
The fern uncurled to look at her, so very fair was she,
with her hair as bright as seaweed new-drawn from out the sea.

By the short cut to Rosses ('twas on the first of May)
I heard the fairies piping, and they piped my heart away;
They piped till I was mad with joy, but when I was alone
I found my heart was piped away and in my breast a stone.

By the short cut to Rosses 'tis I'll go never more,
Lest I be robbed of soul by her that stole my heart before,
Lest she take my soul and crush it like a dead leaf in her hand,
For the short cut to Rosses is the way to Fairyland.

Nora Hopper Chesson: from *Under Quicken Boughs* (1896)

Amhrán na Bealtaine

Focail: Traidisiúnta
Ceol: P.Ní Uallacháin

Allegretto

Bá bóg na Bealtaine maigh dean a'tsamh-raidh

Suas gach cnoc is síos gach gleann

Cail-ín-í mais each-a bán-gheal a gléi geal

Thug a mar féin an samh radh linn

Samh-radh buí ó huí na gréin-e

Thug a mar léin an samh radh linn Ó

bhail e go bail-e-'s'na bhail e'na dhiaidh sin

Thug a mar féin an samh radh linn.

Amhrán na Bealtaine (May Song)

This is a summer carol from Ulster, the music by Pádraigín Ní Uallacháin.

Bábóg na Bealtaine maighdean a' tsamhraidh
Suas gach cnoc is síos gach gleann
Cailíní maiseacha bángheala gléigeal
Thugamar féin samhradh linn.

Samhradh buí ó lui na gréine
Thugamar féin an samhradh linn
Ó bhaile go baile 's 'na bhaile 'na dhiaidh sin
Thugamar féin an samhradh linn

Pronounced:
(babogue na baltana my jan a taurie)
(suas gachnooc is sheas gachglan)
(cahleenee masheeha banyala glaygal)
(hogomar hayn an sauwro lin)

(soaw ro bwee oh looee na grainya)
(hogomar ayn an sowro lin)
(oh walya go bally sna walya na yaishin)
(hogomar hayn an sauwro lin)

Translated, the words mean:

The May Dolly summer maidens go up each hill and down each glen.
Beautiful young girls bright and joyous, bringing the summer garland with us.
Golden summer since sunset, we brought the summer garland with us.
From town to town and home afterwards, we brought the summer garland with us.

The Cuckoo

The cuckoo is a pretty bird, she sings as she flies,
She bringeth good tiding, she telleth no lies
she drinks the rock water to keep her voice clear
And she only calls cuckoo when summer draws near.

The Cuckoo

The cuckoo is a pretty bird, she sings as she flies,
She brings us good tidings, she tells us no lies.
She drinks the rock water to keep her voice clear,
And she never calls 'cuckoo' till the summer draws near.

Festive food

Carrageen (or Irish Moss) is a dark, purplish-red seaweed, flat-stalked with dark, fan-like fronds.

Best harvested in late spring or early summer, it can be gathered from rocks and stones at low tide. It must be washed well with clean water. It can be dried and stored for later use.

To dry it, lay the seaweed on the grass and leave out for about two weeks, sprinkling with water occasionally. Once it has turned a creamy-white colour, it must be dried in sunlight.

Carrageen blancmange

Ingredients:
Shredded rind of one lemon
$1^1/_2$ pints / 845ml milk
2 tbsp honey
$^1/_2$ oz / 13g carrageen moss

Method:
Wash the carrageen moss then place it in a saucepan with the milk and lemon rind.
Bring slowly to the boil then add the honey, stirring till it dissolves.
Strain and pour into a jelly mould or bowl.
Leave to set, then turn it out onto a plate.

Picnic ideas

Wash carrots, apples and celery before you go out. Only cut them into chunky sticks when you sit down for the picnic.

Quick oat and cheese rolls

Ingredients:
8 oz / 225g self-raising flour
4 oz / 110g medium oatmeal
2 tsp baking powder
2 oz / 50g grated cheese
4 tbsp olive oil
1 beaten egg
5 tbsp milk

Method:
This is a quick no-knead bread. Preheat the oven to gas mark 6 (200°C / 400°F).
Sift flour and baking powder into a bowl. Add the grated cheese and oatmeal and mix together.
Beat the milk, olive oil, egg and mustard together.
Pour into the dry ingredients, stirring with a knife, until it forms a soft dough.
Turn out onto a floured surface and cut into eight pieces. Form these into balls and place on a greased baking sheet.
With a sharp knife, cut a cross on the top of each roll.
Bake for 15-20 minutes.

Quiche tartlets

Ingredients:

For the pastry:
4 oz / 110g wholemeal flour
4 oz / 110g white flour
4 oz / 110g vegetable margarine
3-4 tbsp water

For the filling:
4 oz / 110g grated cheese
2 tomatoes
3 eggs
1/2 pint / 275ml milk
Salt and pepper

Method:
Preheat the oven to gas mark 4 (180°C / 350°F). Sift the flour into a bowl. Add the margarine and rub in using the fingertips until it looks like fine breadcrumbs.
Add enough water to make a smooth dough. Roll out the dough on a floured surface.
Cut out circles 10cm / 4 inches in diameter.
Lightly grease a muffin tray. Place a pastry circle in each muffin case.
Put grated cheese into each pastry case, keeping a little aside for topping.
Slice tomatoes thinly. Place one slice into each pastry case.
Beat eggs and milk with salt and pepper. Pour a little into each tart and sprinkle with the remaining cheese.
Bake for 20 minutes until the filling is set. Cool on a wire rack.

Vegetable pasties

Ingredients:
8 oz / 225g shortcrust pastry
2 tbsp oil
1 onion
1 small potato
1 carrot
3 oz broccoli
1 oz / 25g peas
3 oz / 85g grated cheese

Method:
Preheat oven to gas mark 6 (200°C / 400°F).
Finely chop the onion, cut potato into 1cm / ¹/₂ inch dice and grate the carrot.
Heat the oil in a saucepan. Add the chopped onion and cook until soft. Stir in the flour.

Add milk, cheese, carrot, potato, broccoli and peas. Bring to the boil and then reduce heat and cook for 2 minutes, stirring all the while, until the sauce thickens.
Leave aside to cool.
Divide the pastry dough into six pieces. Roll each out to a circle about 16 cm / 6 inches across.
Brush around the edges of the circle with water. Put a portion of the filling in the centre of each pastry circle.
Fold the pastry to form a half moon shape. Press the edges together to seal, using your thumbs.
Place on a greased baking sheet, glaze with milk or a little beaten egg and bake for 25 minutes.

Whitsun

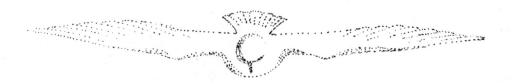

Whitsun, also known as Pentecost, is the seventh Sunday after Easter. It marks the time when the fire of the Holy Spirit descended upon the twelve Apostles, making them speak in such a way that all who heard could understand. The Holy Spirit is often portrayed as a white dove.

In Ireland Whit Sunday was thought to be a dangerous time to go on a journey, particularly by water. It was not a good time to visit the seaside, to swim, sail or even to have a bath.

A person or animal born this day (known as a *cingciseach,* from the Irish word for Pentecost) was thought to be doomed to perform some evil deed. Placing a fly in the baby's hand to be crushed could prevent this bad luck, for having killed something, the child was then freed from its evil fate.

Whit Monday was formerly a favourite day for patterns (a pattern is a patron saint's day, usually marked by fairs and games) and visits to holy wells.

Things to make and do

Whitsun dove

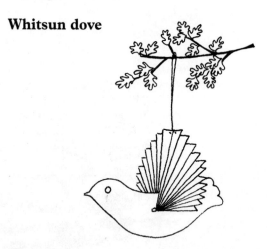

You will need:
White card
White tissue paper
Needle and thread
Scissors or craft knife

148

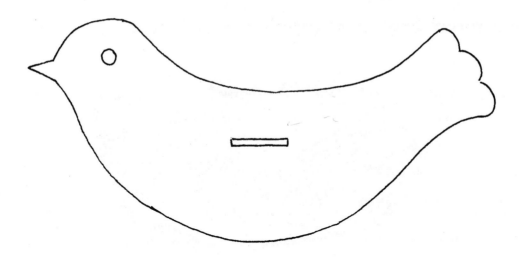

Method:

Copy the dove pattern onto white card and cut it out. Cut a slit for the wings and draw an eye.

Cut a strip of tissue paper 12 x 15cm / 5 x 6 inches.

Place in front of you with the narrower edge facing you. Fold the tissue paper like a fan or concertina, using folds between 1cm and 1.5cms / about ½ inch wide.

Fold the 'fan' in half and insert through the slit in the dove's body until the midpoint is reached.

Spread the wings and join the two together at the top with the needle and thread, leaving a long thread for hanging the bird.

Garlands

Gather white flowers and make a flower garland (see page 134 for details) or a simple daisy chain.

Festive food

Lay a white cloth and light a white candle, dress in white and prepare a white meal.

How many white foods can you think of?

There's yoghurt, potato cakes, rice, pasta, cream, milk, coconut and don't forget meringues and ice cream!

Summer solstice, 21-23 June
Midsummer Day or St John's Day, 24 June

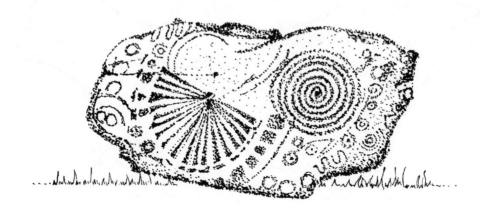

Summer solstice, 21 June, is the longest day of the year. The sun appears to stand still (solstice means 'sun stand'), rising at the same point for three days in a row. The sun is at its zenith at this time, but from now onwards the wheel of the year slowly turns towards the dark again.

Now is the time to celebrate fullness, abundance and the fulfilment of promise, all that has been made manifest in the outer world. We acknowledge that form now on we will start to turn inwards again, into our interior selves. But today, we celebrate nature's great outer light and abundance!

Midsummer's Day has been fixed on 24 June which is also known as St John's Day as it is said to be the birthday of St John the Baptist.

Traditionally a fire was lit at sunset on St John's Eve. Each household lit a small fire quietly at home to bring blessing to their home and family. Later all the inhabitants of the area gathered at a crossroads or other open space for a large community fire.

For days beforehand boys collected firewood to make a brilliant blaze. A prayer or blessing was spoken as the fire was lit. Each person held a handful of smooth round pebbles and walked clockwise around the blaze a prescribed number of times, repeating a prayer. On completing each circuit they threw one pebble into the centre until there were no stones left to keep count.

The fire gave occasion for dancing, singing and feats of strength. Boys extracted burning sticks from the fire to hurl high into the dark night air.

As the fire died down, there was the chance to jump over the embers. Anyone embarking on a new endeavour, or about to go on a journey would jump backwards and forwards over the coals three times.

Others jumped the fire to ensure good health, long life, protection from diseases or the evil eye. Pregnant women stepped over to ensure a safe delivery while young couples jumped hand-in-hand together for luck.

The ashes and embers were thought to have protective properties. Each household took a 'seed' from the fire back to their own hearth. The first fire in a new house had to be lit from the St John's fire. A house mistakenly built on a fairy path could be set to rights by lighting a line of fires from this seed of the St John's fire on the path.

Burning brands were thrown into fields of crops as a blessing and ashes were sprinkled in the four corners of fields. Sometimes a smouldering bush or a torch made of rushes was carried around the fields, reminiscent of the Native American tradition of 'smudging' or smoke-cleansing. Cattle were driven through the fire or singed with embers.

Most of the seasonal festivals have a prohibition on turning a wheel, but at St John's Eve in some places a wooden wheel was set alight and rolled down a hill. Perhaps this was because of the druid Mog Ruith who was said to travel the country at midsummer on a flying wheel.

Midsummer was the time when migrant workers from the north west of Ireland made the journey to Scotland and England for the potato harvest or 'tattie-howking'.

The St John's fire

Today the St John's fires are still lit at crossroads throughout Ireland, though these days the fires are often made up of old tractor tyres and scrap timber.

At Raheen Wood Steiner School in County Clare the children, teachers and parents gather around the St John's fire, which is the last festival of the school year before the summer holidays begin. Everybody comes especially dressed for the occasion in reds, oranges and yellows. As they sing and dance around the fire, the children look like flames themselves.

The fire is lit by the pupils of the oldest class, who will be leaving at the end of the term, ready to move on to secondary school. Everybody takes a bundle of green grass stalks and ties that into a knot, throwing it into the fire with a wish for the future or something they'd like to clear out of their lives.

When the fire has died down, everybody jumps across the embers, even the little ones, who are often helped across by the older children.

The Secrets of Healing

LONG AGO the druid Dian Cecht of the Tuatha De Danaan was known as a great healer. With his children Miach and Airmid he built the wondrous Well of Slaine.

So great was his gift that he could restore to health those of his people who had been wounded in battle. This he did by immersing them in the waters of the healing well from which they emerged whole and renewed as if reborn from the womb of all life.

Nuada, the king of the Tuatha De Danaan, had been severely wounded in the first battle of Moytura, his hand being severed at the wrist. The law of the people said that no one could rule over the Tuatha De Danaan who was not whole himself. Dian Cecht fashioned for Nuada a hand of silver and so Nuada was restored and all seemed well, the hand performing the functions of a normal hand.

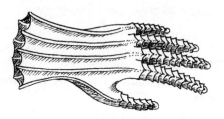

Miach and Airmid travelled the country performing acts of healing as they wandered where their gifts were needed. One day as they arrived at the gates to Nuada's stronghold they found that the guard on duty had lost an eye in a recent skirmish.

'A guard needs two good eyes to mind his master's gates,' said Miach. 'Let me see how I can help you.'

So Miach took an eye from a cat and fixed it into the guard's eye socket and thus restored his sight. The guard was delighted. That is, he was until his new eye kept him awake at night searching for mice.

Wishing to be of service to his king, Miach approached Nuada saying, 'Sire, I hear the silver hand troubles you at times. I promise you that I can give you a hand that will surpass that my father has fashioned for you. I can restore your own hand that was cut off and make you whole once more.'

'Do not listen to him, my king, for he knows not what he says,' roared Dian Cecht. 'He is a foolish boy who knows how to take an eye out of a cat, but cannot take the cat out of the eye!'

The king agreed to let Miach attempt to restore his severed hand. And so the hand was brought to Miach who cleaned it well and set to work with his herbs and incantations. Three days and nights he worked with the hand bound by the king's side till new flesh covered the bones. Three days more he worked with it bound by Nuada's heart till blood flowed in its veins and three days more till its life, strength and movement were fully recovered. At last, the hand was perfect in every way.

Dian Cecht was furious to be thus outshone by his own son. 'So, you think you are a greater healer than I? Then show me how you can heal this!' Saying this, Dian Cecht took up his sword and struck Miach on the forehead, cutting through the skin.

From this Miach quickly healed. Dian Cecht took his sword once more and smote him, this time cutting through to the bone. Again Miach healed his own wound.

A third time, Dian Cecht struck his son, this time until Miach's brain could be seen in the wound, and again Miach healed himself.

At last Dian Cecht could take no more. In a fury he raised his sword once more and struck with all his strength, till his son's head was split in two. This wound Miach could not heal, nor Airmid his sister with all her skills. Even Dian Cecht himself could not heal this wound, and stood shocked at what he had done.

Airmid removed her green cloak and laid it tenderly over her beloved brother's body, singing softly and strewing him with flowers. Each day for a year she came to sit by his grave, adding a handful of soil to the grave mound.

When spring brought the promise of new growth, green shoots pushed through the blanket of earth over Miach's body and as they grew each took on a different shape and colouring.

At length 365 green herbs and healing plants covered the mound and where each grew that was the part of the body for which it was a remedy.

Once more Airmid took off her cloak and laid it on the ground by Miach's grave. She plucked each herb and laid it carefully on her green mantle, noting its position and recording its usage, 'Coltsfoot on the chest has a cure for lung complaints. Hawthorn for the heart, peppermint for the stomach, comfrey for bones, lavender for ...'

When Dian Cecht saw that Airmid meant to preserve the wisdom of the healing herbs his fury returned once more. 'What, even in death is Miach the greater healer? And you Airmid, would you give mankind these secrets? This shall not be. Some mysteries must remain!'

Dian Cecht caught up the mantle and shook it so that the herbs were scattered to the four winds. And so the knowledge of healing was lost to the people who ever after have sought to recover it and make themselves whole once more.

The following folk song refers to the time of romances among young people, when they were moving with the cattle to the summer pastures.

Wild Mountain Thyme

*O the summertime is coming
And the wee birds sweetly singing
And the wild mountain thyme
Grows around the blooming heather.*

Chorus:
*Will ye go, lassie go, and we'll all go together
To pull wild mountain thyme
All around the blooming heather.
Will ye go, lassie go?*

*I will build my love a bower
By yon clear crystal fountain
And around it I will pile
All the flowers of the mountain*

Chorus

*If my true love she won't go,
I will surely find another
Where the wild mountain thyme
Grows around the blooming heather.*

Chorus

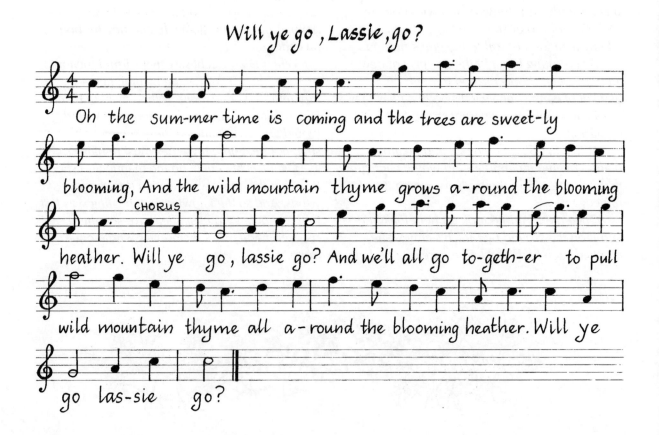

Will ye go, Lassie, go?

Oh the sum-mer time is coming and the trees are sweet-ly blooming, And the wild mountain thyme grows a-round the blooming heather. Will ye go, lassie go? And we'll all go to-geth-er to pull wild mountain thyme all a-round the blooming heather. Will ye go las-sie go?

Games

This is good time for playing outdoor games and sports of all kinds. See the Bealtaine and Lughnasadh sections for suggestions for these. Also appropriate to this time would be turning cartwheels, races of all kinds and feats of strength such as sheaf-tossing and tug-o-war, and tests of skill such as wellie-throwing and Beat the Goalie.

Fair Rosa

This is a traditional children's ring game from the north of Ireland based on the story of Sleeping Beauty, otherwise known as Briar Rose or Fair Rosa.

The children stand in a circle holding hands. Three are picked to play the three main characters, Fair Rosa, Ugly Fay and the Prince. The song begins with Fair Rosa standing alone in the ring. The actions for each verse are shown in italics below the words.

Fair Rosa was a lovely child, a lovely child,
a lovely child
Fair Rosa was a lovely child, long long ago.
(Fair Rosa stands alone within the ring of
    children holding hands and walking round
    to the left.)

One day there came an ugly Fay, ugly Fay,
ugly Fay, etc
(Ugly Fay steps into the ring)

The Ugly Fay gave her a rose, her a rose,
her a rose, etc
(Ugly Fay and Rosa shake hands then Ugly
    Fay rejoins the ring)

She pricked her finger on the rose, on the rose,
on the rose, etc

She fell asleep a hundred years, a hundred years,
a hundred years, etc
(Rosa lies on the ground)

The briars they grew all around, all around,
all around, etc
(The children all crowd in around Rosa)

A handsome prince came riding by, riding by,
riding by, etc
(The Prince walks around the outside of the
   circle)

He cut the briars one by one, one by one,
one by one, etc
(The Prince makes the action of cutting the
   briars with his sword)

He kissed Fair Rosa's lily-white hand,
lily-white hand, lily-white hand, etc
(Prince enters circle, bends down to kiss
   Rosa's hand)

Fair Rosa is a happy bride, happy bride,
happy bride, etc.
(Rosa and Prince stand holding hands in the
   centre of the circle.)

The game can continue with another three
children chosen to play the main characters.

Fair Rosa

Fair Rosa was a love-ly child, a love-ly child, a love-ly child. Fair Rosa was a love-ly child, a long time a-go.

Festive food

Elderflower pancakes

Ingredients:
4 oz / 110g flour
1 egg
1/2 pint / 275ml milk
Pinch salt
A few heads of elderflowers
Sunflower oil to deep fry
Clear honey or castor sugar
Lemon

Method:
Beat eggs, milk, flour and salt to make
  a batter.
Holding the elderflowers by the stalk, dip
  into the batter.

Deep fry in hot sunflower oil until brown.
Drain on kitchen paper and cut off the stalk.
  Dust with castor sugar or drizzle with
  clear honey. Add a squirt of lemon juice.

Elderflower 'champagne'

Ingredients:
7-10 elderflower heads
1 1/2 lb / 750g sugar
2 tbsp cider vinegar
1 gallon / 4.5 litres cold water
2 lemons

Method:
Fill a large, food-quality plastic bucket with
  water. Add the elderflowers, sugar,
  vinegar, lemon juice and rind (without the
  white part).

Cover with a tea towel and leave to stand for
  24 hours.
Strain through muslin and pour into
  sterilised screw top bottles.

This delicious summer refresher will be
ready to drink in three weeks. As it will keep
well stored in a cool, dark place, you can
make enough to last throughout the summer.

Herb butter

Ingredients:
4 oz / 110g butter
1 tsp thyme
1 tsp parsley
1 clove garlic

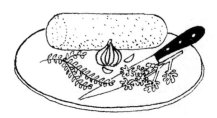

Method:
Finely chop the thyme and parsley and crush
  the garlic.
Soften the butter and beat in the herbs.
  Allow the butter to harden and form into
  a sausage shape.
Wrap in greaseproof paper and store in the
  fridge.
Cut into slices and use with French bread or
  vegetables.

Bouquet garni

Ingredients:
Sprig of thyme
Sprig of parsley
1 bay leaf
2 peppercorns
10cm / 4 inch square of fine muslin

Method:
Place sprigs of thyme, parsley, the bay leaf and peppercorns in the centre of a square of muslin.
Bring all four corners of the square together and tie with cotton to form a little bag.
Add this to soups and stews for flavour and remove it before serving.

Tasty herb stuffing

Ingredients:
1 onion
1 oz / 25g butter
4 oz / 110g wholemeal bread
1 tbsp chopped parsley
1 tbsp chopped thyme
1 beaten egg
Juice and grated rind of 1/2 lemon
Salt and pepper

Method:
Finely chop the onion and fry in the butter until soft but not brown.
Make breadcrumbs by crumbling the bread or putting it through a mincer or grinder.

Mix the breadcrumbs with the onions in a bowl. Add the chopped herbs, lemon juice and rind, and salt and pepper to taste.
Add the beaten egg and mix well.

This stuffing is delicious in a vegetarian nut roast, in baked trout or in the more traditional chicken or turkey.

Herbs

St John's Day was known as the best time to gather many herbs whilst their properties were at their height. Many common wild herbs are at their best at this time: elderflowers, yarrow, peppermint, St John's Wort, while cultivated herbs such as lemon balm and lavender are also ready to harvest. The wild rose is in bloom.

Pick herbs before noon on a dry sunny day from areas away from traffic and agricultural chemicals.

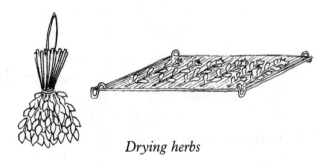

Drying herbs

To dry, hang in bunches or lay on a cake cooling rack in single layers.

Store dried herbs in coloured glass jars.

Herbal teas

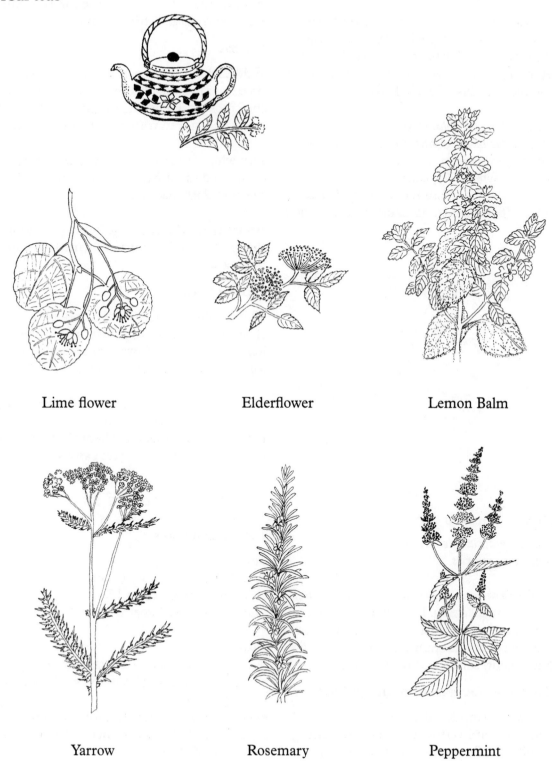

Lime flower   Elderflower   Lemon Balm

Yarrow   Rosemary   Peppermint

St John's Wort *(Hypericum perforatum)*

This was known as the fairy herb and was said to protect against witchcraft. It is used to treat wounds, burns, bruises, sunburn and rheumatics. Here is an invocation spoken while picking this valuable herb:

St John's Wort, St John's Wort,
Blessed is the one who has you in his possession
I harvest you with my right hand
I store you with my left hand.
from the Carmina Gadelica,
(collected by Alexander Carmichael)

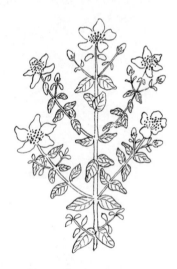

St John's Wort Oil

For neuralgia, shingles, nerve pains, burns, wounds and injuries

Pick the flowering tops, including the highest leaves and small stems. Place them in a jar and cover with olive oil. Leave the jar in a sunny place for about a month, until the oil is quite red in colour. Strain and bottle the oil.

Elderflower, peppermint and yarrow

Mix equal quantities of elderflower, peppermint and yarrow to make a remedy for colds and flu. For an infusion, add 2 teaspoons of the dried herbs to a cup of boiling water. Leave to infuse for 10 minutes, strain and drink 3 times a day.

Thyme

Wild thyme is common throughout Ireland on dry grasslands, heaths, sand dunes and in the cracks in limestone pavements. It can be dried and stored with little loss of flavour.

Dry whole branches of thyme, removing leaves and discarding the stems once dried. Store in dark glass jars.

An infusion of thyme is good for a cold in the chest. Use 2 tsp dried thyme to a cup of boiling water.

Herbal baths

The addition of herbs can turn a bath into a relaxing treat. Add an infusion of lavender, lemon balm, elderflowers or rosemary leaves for a relaxing and beautifully scented bath.

During teething or for a child who just cannot get to sleep, an infusion of chamomile or lime flowers can be added to a bedtime bath. If you don't have fresh herbs you can use teabags.

Things to make and do

Lavender favour

You will need:
An odd number of long stems of fresh
    lavender, 11, 13, or 15
Narrow ribbon, 1 metre

Method:
Tie the ribbon just below the flower heads,
    leaving one end about 25cm / 10 inches
    long.
Bend each stem carefully over the flowers so
    that the flowers are concealed within the
    bunch of stems.

Hide the short ribbon among the stems.

Weave the longer ribbon in and out through the stems until the flowers are hidden.

Wrap the ribbon tightly around the bundle a few times.

Pull the shorter ribbon out from among the stalks and finish off by tying the two ribbons in a decorative bow.

This 'favour' can be hung in a wardrobe to keep moths away from good clothes, hung near your pillow to aid sleep, or displayed in a vase.

Method:

Dry the sage by hanging in bunches in a warm and airy place.

When dry, gather a bundle of sage stems together, about 15cm / 6 inches in length.

Bind well with cotton.

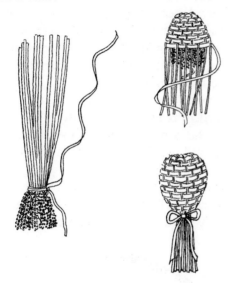

Sage smudging stick

In older times a smoking branch was carried around the fields to cleanse and purify them and bring a blessing to the crops. This appears similar to the Native American custom of 'smudging' or cleansing with the smoke from burning sage.

You can make your own smudge stick using home-grown sage.

You will need:
Between 6 and 12 stems of fresh sage
Cotton yarn

To use the smudge stick

Light one end of the smudge stick and allow the flames to go out. Waft the smoke from the smouldering herbs above your head, down the length of your body, under your feet, around your back, allowing it to fill and cleanse the energetic aura that surrounds your physical body. Having cleansed yourself with the smoke, you can now bring the sage smoke around the corners of your house, garden or fields.

Rose petal tincture

To mend a broken heart

You will need:
1 part rose petals
3 parts Vodka

Method:
On St John's Day in the morning, pick the petals from scented garden roses. Maintain an attitude of listening, and allow the flowers to speak to you. Let them tell you which flowers to pick and which to leave.

Put the petals in a clear glass jar. Pour in vodka to cover the petals. Screw on the lid and shake well.

Leave for two weeks in a dark place, shaking it once every day.

To heal a broken heart, take 20 drops of rose petal tincture twice a day.

Mandalas

Mandalas are circular patterns that can be found in the art of most spiritual traditions. The Sanskrit word mandala means both circle and centre. Making a mandala can be a meditative experience through which we come to understand our place in the universe. We can also simply celebrate the beauty and fun of making a mandala. Many Celtic designs lend themselves to mandala-making.

Sunwheel mandala

You will need:
Red lentils
Millet
White rice
Square of hardboard

Method:
Copy the pattern for the triple spiral sunwheel to the size you want (using a photocopier you can either reduce or enlarge the design). Trace this pattern onto the flat surface of the hardboard with a pencil.

Fill up each segment of the sunwheel with grains, using the different colours to create a beautiful pattern.

Having completed the mandala, allow yourself to really see the pattern there. Then you can pour the grains off the board and use them again to make a different pattern.

If you would like to preserve your mandala, you can coat each section of the mandala with PVA glue before adding the grains.

Earth art mandalas

Having mastered this technique, you can move onto bigger things, creating mandalas outside on the ground.

At the beach, make a mandala of rounded pebbles, driftwood, found objects and sand.

In the woods, use pinecones, feathers and leaves to make a mandala on the forest floor.

In your garden, make a mandala of flowers, stones, gravel, twigs and roots on the grass.

The possibilities for outdoor mandalas are as endless as your imagination.

Spectacular sun fire wheel

★★★
Safety warning – this activity is for adults only!
★★★

This is an activity that can be prepared during the day in readiness for the evening's celebration. The wheel is set alight after dark. While it is spectacular for children to watch, it is not appropriate for them to prepare!

You will need:
An open space
An old bicycle or pram wheel
5m / 5½ yards light fencing wire
Electric drill
Old sheets
15cm / 6 inch nail
Fencepost
Paraffin

Method:
The bicycle wheel forms the body of the sun wheel. The fencing wire is used to make the rays of the sun.

To make the fuse:
Tear the sheets into strips about 15cm / 6 inches wide.

Bend the fencing wire in half around a nail in the wall. Insert the two ends to the chuck of an electric drill, inserting the rags in between the two wires.

Start to twist it while holding the loose end of the sheet between the wires. Twist the wires together until the whole length is fairly even at about 20 to 15 twists per 10 centimetres.

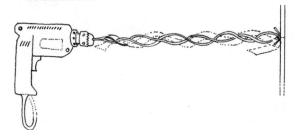

Remove from the drill and nail. You now have a strong wire bound with rags.

Form the wire into the shape of the rays of the sun. Do this one ray at a time and tie in place on the wheel with fencing wire.

Attach the wheel to a fencepost using a 5cm / 6-inch nail through the central mechanism.

Dowse the rags with paraffin, being very careful that there are no sparks or flames nearby and making sure not to spill any on your clothing.

Spin the wheel. Using a long taper or torch from the fire, set the wheel alight in several places at once.

Stand well back and be amazed as you watch the sun's turning.

12 July

On the morning of 12 July, Orangemen, smartly dressed in dark suits, sashes and bowler hats, march in processions led by colourful banners, with bands playing flutes and drums – including the famously huge Lambeg drum. The Orange Order has a number of community halls and each hall has its own flute band and its own banner.

The marches begin at the church, proceed around the boundary of the community and meet up with other bands at a field outside town, where community leaders give speeches.

The marching season begins with the Apprentice Boys of Derry parade on Easter Monday and continues through the summer to the last Saturday in September. The 12 July march is the biggest and best known.

12 July is celebrated in the north of Ireland by members of the Protestant community. It commemorates the Battle of the Boyne, when King William of Orange won a battle against King James VII and II in 1690, which ended Catholic supremacy in the British Isles.

Despite its sectarian and political nature, the parades held by members of the Orange Order in many parts of Ulster were once said to be some of the most colourful and festive days in the local rural calendar.

Huge bonfires are lit throughout the North, but especially in Belfast on the night of 11 July. Each housing estate has its own bonfires. Local youths gather firewood and try to have the biggest bonfire in the area, guarding their supplies against theft by youths from the next street.

In Scarva, near Portadown, on 13 July there is a mock battle between two horsemen dressed as William of Orange and James II. William, of course, always wins.

The Ould Orange Flute

Words: Nugent Bohem
Air: 'Toor-al-ay'

In the County Ty-rone near the town of Dunganon, Where many's a ruction myself had a hand in, Bob Williamson lived a weaver by trade And as all of us thought him a stout Orange Blade On the twelfth of Ju-ly as it yearly did come, Bob played on the flute to the sound of the drum. You may talk of your harp, your pi-an-o or lute, but there's nothing could sound like the ould orange flute. Tour-al-u, tour-al-ay Singin' toor-al-ay, Toor-al-ay oor-al-ay aah.

The Old Orange Flute

In the County Tyrone, in the town of Dungannon
Where many a ruckus myself had a hand in
Bob Williamson lived there, a weaver by trade
And all of us thought him a stout-hearted blade.

12 July

On the twelfth of July as it yearly did come
Bob played on the flute to the sound of the drum
You can talk of your fiddles, your harp or your lute
But there's nothing could sound like the Old Orange Flute.

But the treacherous scoundrel, he took us all in
For he married a Papist named Bridget McGinn
Turned Papish himself and forsook the Old Cause
That gave us our freedom, religion and laws.

And the boys in the county made such a stir on it
They forced Bob to flee to the province of Connaught;
Took with him his wife and his fixins, to boot,
And along with the rest went the Old Orange Flute.

Each Sunday at mass, to atone for past deeds,
Bob said Paters and Aves and counted his beads
Till one Sunday morn, at the priest's own require
Bob went for to play with the flutes in the choir.

He went for to play with the flutes in the mass
But the instrument quivered and cried, "O Alas!"
And blow as he would, though he made a great noise,
The flute would play only "The Protestant Boys".

Bob jumped up and huffed, and was all in a flutter.
He pitched the old flute in the best holy water;
He thought that this charm would bring some other sound,
When he tried it again, it played "Croppies Lie Down!"

And for all he would finger and twiddle and blow
For to play Papish music, the flute would not go;
"Kick the Pope" to "Boyne Water" was all it would sound
Not one Papish bleat in it could e'er be found.

At a council of priests that was held the next day
They decided to banish the Old Flute away;
They couldn't knock heresy out of its head
So they bought Bob another to play in its stead.

And the Old Flute was doomed, and its fate was pathetic
'Twas fastened and burnt at the stake as heretic.
As the flames rose around it, you could hear a strange noise
'Twas the Old Flute still a-whistlin' "The Protestant Boys".

Papist = a Roman Catholic

167

BEING something of an unrepentant rogue I have always enjoyed the spectacle of the community festival, even if the celebration was in honour of something I was not supposed to enjoy! To be specific, I was brought up in the sectarian North of Ireland as a Roman Catholic. Hand on heart, I always thought the Protestants put on the best community festivals even if that was to celebrate the burning of Guy Fawkes or the Pope! I would sneak out under penalty of death by my parents and excommunication by the Church and wander through the waves of pipe playing, banner bawling 'Proddies' and be thrilled by the fabulous cavalcade of music and drama that I still call today 'festivals to die for'.

Alexander Mackenzie

Summer to Autumn

Lughnasadh

Lughnasadh

(pronounced loonassah)

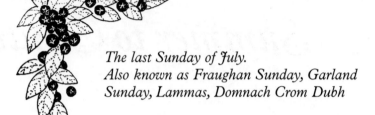

The last Sunday of July.
Also known as Fraughan Sunday, Garland
Sunday, Lammas, Domnach Crom Dubh

The festival of Lughnasadh is named after the sun god Lugh who held funeral games at this time of year for his foster mother Tailtu. Tailtu died after her exertions in clearing the forests of the central plain of Ireland ready for cultivation.

Lughnasadh marks the beginning of the harvest and the beginning of the end of the summer.

Traditionally this was only the beginning of two weeks of festivities. Nowadays, celebrations take place on the last Sunday in July. This day is known by many names, which tell a little about the customs associated with it:

Garland Sunday – wildflower garlands were made and worn by the girls, also to decorate holy wells and stone circles, notably the largest stone in the biggest stone circle in Ireland, by Lough Gur in County Limerick.

Height Sunday – the whole community would together climb the highest hill in the area. Each area of the country had its own special mountain, such as Mount Brandon in Kerry and Croagh Padraig in Mayo. Croagh Padraig is still the site of a pilgrimage today, many people choosing to climb the mountain barefoot as a penance.

Fraughan Sunday – fraughan is the Gaelic word for the bilberry. The young people would go out to gather bilberries on the high moors. It was a time for courting, and the boys would give their bilberries to their chosen sweetheart who would bake a cake for sharing at the dance that evening.

Domhnach Crom Dubh – Crom Dubh, the 'dark crooked one', brought the secrets of cultivation to the Irish. As he was said to live on a high hill, the first corn of the harvest was taken to a high place and buried there in his honour. He was overcome by Lugh, the young, bright god who brought new knowledge.

Lammas – Lammas comes from the old English 'Loaf Mass' a celebration of the ripening of the grain. The Old Lammas Fair in Ballycastle, County Antrim, is well known.

Lughnasadh traditions abound, including the holding of fairs and assemblies *(aonach)*, particularly horse fairs. It was a time for horse racing and for swimming the horses through a river to receive a cleansing and blessing from the element of water, in the same way that cattle were driven between the fires at Bealtaine and, later, St John's. There would be games and trials of strength, trading of goods, entertainment and the spreading of news and gossip.

The Story of Lugh

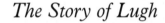

*L*ONG AGO, *in Ireland, King Bres the Fomorian ruled over the land. His was a harsh and brutal rule and the people went hungry for many years. The earth was blighted and famine was widespread throughout the land.*

The Tuatha De Danaan, people of the goddess Danu, were miserable and hungry, and longed to overturn this merciless king. But Bres could not be overthrown so long as his champion Balor of the evil eye was alive. It was said that one man alone might slay Balor – his own grandson. To safeguard against that day, Balor imprisoned his daughter Ethlinn in a tower where she was hidden from the world and no man could see her beauty.

One day Cian, the son of Dian Cecht the chief druid of the Tuatha De Danaan, was sent as an emissary to the Fomorians, to the northerly fortress of Balor on the high cliffs. Amongst his many talents, Cian had the magical ability to open any lock.

One day he heard the voice of a maiden singing sweet and low from a tall tower. The stout oak door swung open at his touch and he followed the notes of her song to the highest tower. Pushing aside the embroidered curtain, he saw a maid in a gown of russet velvet that matched the fire of her hair. She was surely the most beautiful maid he had ever seen.

Each day Cian went secretly to be with her and a deep love grew between them. When a child was born, fair of face and shining like the morning, Eithlinn said 'Let us call him Lugh, that he may bring some light to this dark world.'

Now it happened that one day Balor heard the cries of the baby come from the tower and realised he had been cheated. In a great rage, he tore the boy Lugh from his mother's arms and hurled him into the white-topped waves below the cliffs to drown.

But all was not lost, no, for the seals of the northern sea found him, this strange shining pup, afloat on the stormy waters, and carried him with them over the waves to the palace of Mananan Mac Lir, Lord of the Sea. In Tir na Nog Lugh grew, day by day taller and more beautiful.

He learned the names and the language of the seals and all the other beasts. He raced the white horses of Mananan's waves to shore, and sometimes he even got there first! He learned the skills of poetry and sorcery, of smithcraft and music, the crafts of the warrior and of healing, and he was happy.

At last, almost full-grown, he remembered the land of Ireland, and wished with all his heart to return.

'What, would you leave this land, where you have never known sorrow, but only joy?' Mananan asks.

'But, foster-father, I can remember green hills and woods and rivers. I hear them whisper my name, and call me, "Lugh! Champion of the Light, come back to Ireland." I must go.'

Mananan replied, 'Much have I loved you, Lugh, son of Cian, and fain would I lose your company. But this day I knew must come. Here, take from me this parting gift, the Sword of Light.'

He strapped over Lugh's heart a breastplate of shining silver and placed on his head a helmet shining like the sun. Into his right hand, he placed the Sword, saying, 'Go now to Ireland with my blessing and protection, and drive the Fomorians from the land of the Tuatha de Danaan.'

Riding on the white sea foam, Lugh came to shore and, passing over hills and through forests, set out for Tara, to take up his place among the Tuatha De Danaan and fulfil his destiny. He reached Nuada's stronghold as dusk was falling and rapped upon the gate, calling, 'Open up and let me in. I am here to lead you in battle against the Fomorians.'

The guard laughed roughly, saying, 'What foolish youth is this? What skill have you brought to Nuada's dun, that we do not already have here?'

'I bring the craft of poetry I learned from my foster-father Mananan Mac Lir.'

'Go away, boy, we have a fine poet within these stout walls.'

'I bring the craft of metalwork that I learned beyond the waves'

'Try again, boy. We already have the greatest smith in all Ireland.'

'I bring the craft of a warrior.'

'We have many warriors within these walls, all mightier that you, puny youth!'

'I bring the craft of the harper.'

'We have a harper and the finest of harpers he is.'

'Then, go ask your chief if he has one man who is skilled in all the crafts!'

The guard hurried away to tell Nuada about the proud boy at the gate, who would not be put off. He returned moments later, to open the gate and bring him to Nuada's hall.

'Welcome samildanach – the many-gifted one! Welcome to this house of heroes. From your face and your valour, you can be none other than Lugh, the son of Cian, grandson of Balor of the one eye. Come, feast with us and tell us of your journey.'

And after the feasting and the singing and the storytelling was over, and it took a great long time, as you might guess, Nuada rose to his feet and said, 'Now, at last, we are ready to rise against the Fomorians. At first light we leave for Moytura and victory!'

On the plain of Moytura, the Tuatha De Danaan met with the Fomorians and a great battle ensued. Many were killed before Balor uncovered his single, deathly eye and turned it

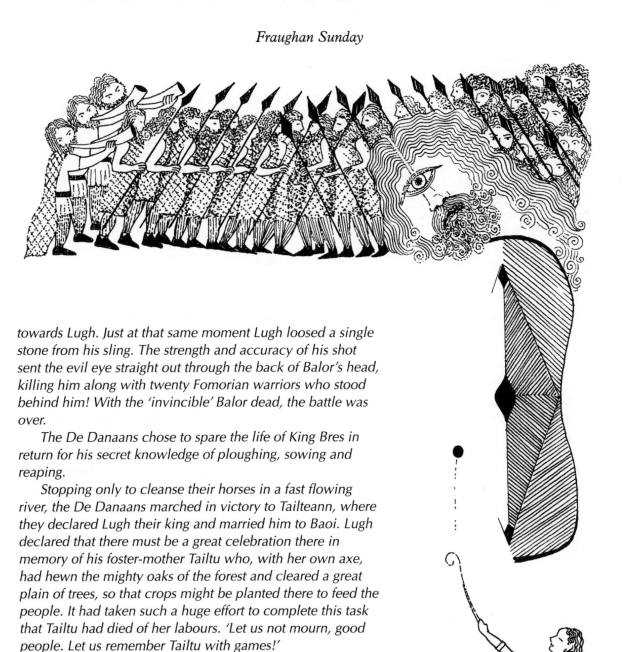

towards Lugh. Just at that same moment Lugh loosed a single stone from his sling. The strength and accuracy of his shot sent the evil eye straight out through the back of Balor's head, killing him along with twenty Fomorian warriors who stood behind him! With the 'invincible' Balor dead, the battle was over.

The De Danaans chose to spare the life of King Bres in return for his secret knowledge of ploughing, sowing and reaping.

Stopping only to cleanse their horses in a fast flowing river, the De Danaans marched in victory to Tailteann, where they declared Lugh their king and married him to Baoi. Lugh declared that there must be a great celebration there in memory of his foster-mother Tailtu who, with her own axe, had hewn the mighty oaks of the forest and cleared a great plain of trees, so that crops might be planted there to feed the people. It had taken such a huge effort to complete this task that Tailtu had died of her labours. 'Let us not mourn, good people. Let us remember Tailtu with games!'

And so people came from all four corners of Ireland for the games on the great plain of Tailtu. There were races on foot and on horseback, races on land and races through lakes and rivers; they played tug-of-war and throwing the hammer; there were contests of song and poetry and magic and the feasting went on for fourteen days and nights.

And still to this day, a great gathering is held each year at Tailteann to celebrate the festival of Lughnasadh.

Frolic

The children were shouting together
And racing along the sands,
A glimmer of dancing shadows,
A dovelike flutter of hands.

The stars were shouting in heaven,
The sun was chasing the moon:
The game was the same as the children's,
They danced to the self-same tune.

The whole of the world was merry,
One joy from the vale to the height,
Where the blue woods of twilight encircled
The lovely lawns of the light.

AE (George Russell)

Things to make

Pocket Lady's apron

You will need:
Apron: 63 x 63cm / 24 x 24 inches cotton
    fabric in colour A
Pockets: 52 x 39cm / 20 x 15 inches cotton
    fabric in colour B
Waistband: 150 x 10cm / 60 x 4 inches
    cotton fabric in colour B
Matching threads
Scissors
Needle and pins
Tailor's chalk

Method:
1. Cut out a rectangle 63 x 63cm from
   fabric A for the skirt of the apron. With
   chalk, make a mark at the mid point of
   the top edge (X). Mark both sides at
   12cm, 27cm and 43cm (5, 11 and 17
   inches) from the top edge.
2. Fold in 0.5cm / ¼ inch on sides and
   bottom edge. Iron. Trim corners and fold
   in another 1cm / ½ inch on these edges.
   Iron and sew in place.
3. Cut out 3 strips 52 x 13cm (20 x 5 inches)
   from fabric B for the pockets. Trim the
   corners.
4. Fold in 1cm / ½ inch on each edge of the
   pocket strips. Iron. Fold in another 1cm /
   ½ inch on the top edge and sew the top
   edge only.
5. Place the top of the first row of pockets at
   the 12cm / 5 inch mark on the apron,
   leaving a gap of 5cm / 2 inches at each
   side. Pin and sew in place being careful to
   leave the top edge open. Place the second
   row of pockets at the 27cm / 11 inch mark
   and the third row at 43cm / 17 inches
   from the top of the apron. Sew in place.
6. To make individual pockets: mark pocket
   strips at 10cm / 4 inch intervals. Pin and
   sew to apron with two lines of stitching.
7. Gather the top edge of the apron into soft
   pleats with large running stitches.
8. Cut a strip of fabric B 150 x 10cm (60 x 4
   inches) for the waistband. Fold in 0.5cm /
   ¼ inch on both long sides and iron.

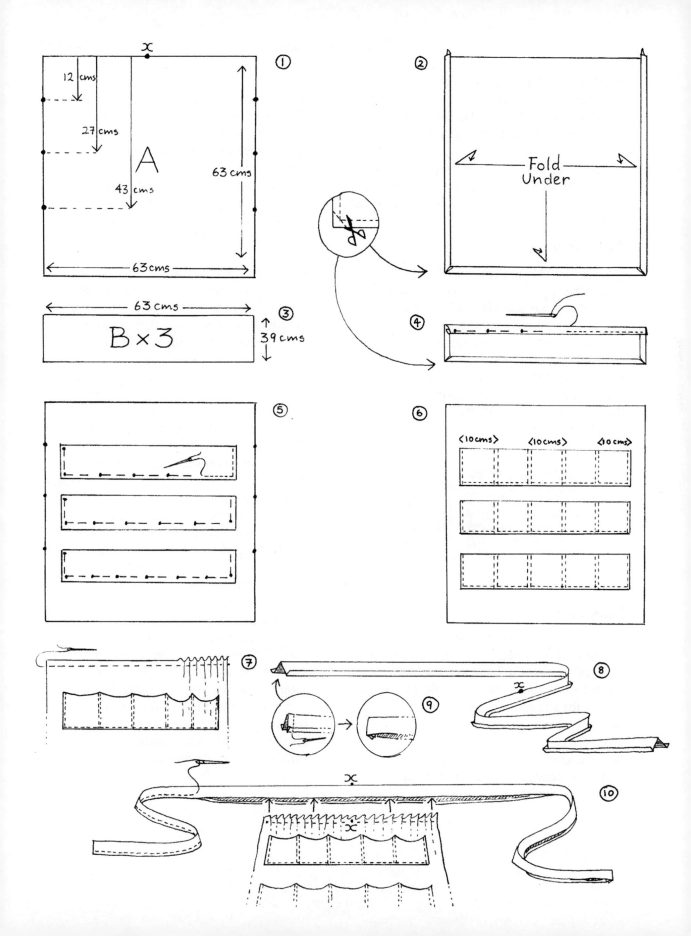

9. Fold waistband in half with right sides together and iron again. Sew short edges together, trim seam and turn the right way out. Mark the mid point of the waistband with chalk (X).

10. Insert gathered edge of apron into the waistband, matching points X. Pin and tack in place. Sew the entire length of the waistband.

Berry picking

This is the time to pick the soft fruits – raspberries, gooseberries, blackcurrants. If you haven't got a garden, why not spend a day in the countryside in search of wild fruits or visit one of the 'pick-your-own-fruit' establishments? Then you can use the fruits of your labours to make jams and jellies, cakes and muffins, puddings or just enjoy them on their own with fresh cream. Mmmm.

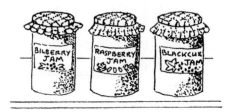

Fairy basket

Young people out berry picking often made a simple basket of rushes to carry home the fruits of the season. Here are instructions for a small rush basket that will hold just enough berries for a fairy's tea party.

You will need:
At least 12 rushes
10cm / 4 inches thread or thin string
Scissors or penknife

Method:
Take four rushes and trim them to the same length, approximately 25cm / 10 inches. Tie these together at their mid point with a little thread. Spread the rushes evenly to form a star.

Take one long thin rush and fold it in half. Place this loop around one of the legs of the star. This becomes the 'weaver' and is woven in the following way (called 'pairing').

Take the front end of the weaver round in front of the leg of the star. Then fold the back end of the weaver over this. This creates a twisted weave that holds the rushes firmly together. Continue in this way around the circle.

Introduce new rushes when needed, matching thick end to thick, thin end to thin.

Gently curve the legs to form the sloping sides of the basket. When the basket is big enough, stop weaving. Poke the last two weavers down along the legs (as shown).

Choose two legs that are opposite each other to become the basket's handle. Trim the other legs to points. Fold each over and push down through the weaving to finish off neatly. Pull and then cut off the excess.

To make the handle, overlap the two remaining legs to form a curve. For a simple handle you could tie these together with a piece of thread.

For a stronger handle, take one more strong rush. Poke one end down alongside one of the legs forming the handle. Twist it around the two overlapping rushes over and over again. Finish off by poking down beside the other leg of the handle. Trim off the excess and any rushes that are sticking out of the basket.

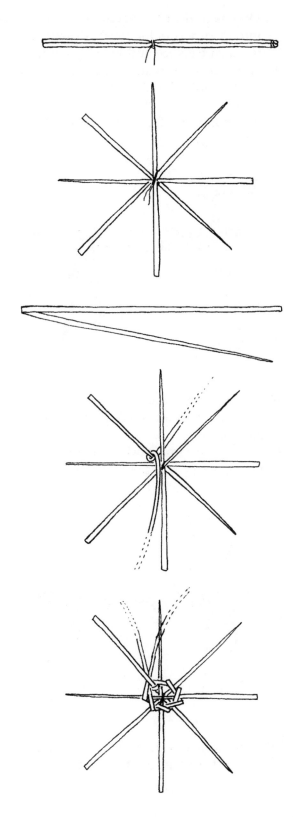

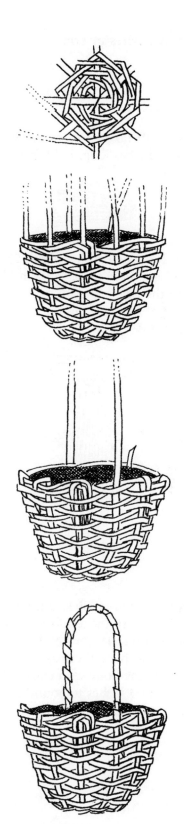

A horse of rushes or straw

You will need:
About 16 rushes or straws

Method:

Horse's head: take 4 rushes cut to about 10cm / 4 inches long. Fold these in half together.

Front body: take 4 rushes about 25cm / 10 inches long. Fold these in the middle around the head.
Tie a piece of rush around the neck to hold it in place.

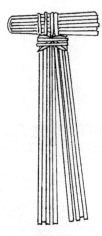

Body: take six more rushes, a little longer, about 35cm / 16 inches. Fold in the middle around the front body.
Bind in place with another rush and crisscross along the body with rushes, leaving about 7cm / 3 inches unbound to form the back legs and tail.

Back legs and tail: separate the body rushes into three sets of four rushes each, i.e. four for each back leg and four for the tail.
Bend the legs down and bind each with a rush to hold. Trim legs to the same length.
Leave four rushes free as the horse's tail. Trim these.

Front legs: form the front legs by splitting the front body rushes into sets of four rushes.
Bind each leg with a rush to hold and trim to the same length as the back legs.

Trim the rushes at the back of the head and spread these out to form a mane.

Festive food

Fraughan (bilberry) fool

Ingredients:
Fraughans – 2 cups
Caster sugar to taste
Whipped cream
  – 1 cup

Method:
Crush the berries with a potato
  masher. Sweeten to taste with
  caster sugar. Fold in the whipped
  cream. Serve in small dishes.

Raspberry vinegar

Ingredients:
2 pints / 1150ml fresh raspberries
1 pint / 570ml cider vinegar
Brown sugar

Method:
Squash the raspberries with a wooden spoon
  in a china bowl. Pour over the vinegar and
  stir well. Cover with a cloth and leave to
  sit for 4 or 5 days, stirring well each day.
Strain through a jelly bag.★ To every cup of
  liquid, add 1/2 cup of sugar.
Heat for 10-15 minutes.
When the mixture has cooled, pour into
  bottles to store.
Dilute one part vinegar to five parts
  lemonade for a refreshing summer drink.
Diluted with hot water, it makes a soothing

drink when you have a cold – a soothing
reminder of warmer days.

★ A 'jelly bag' is a muslin or nylon bag for
  straining jams and jellies through.

Raspberry jam

Ingredients:
1 lb / 450g raspberries
1 lb / 450g sugar

Method:
Heat the raspberries until they begin to boil.
  Add the sugar, which has been heated in
  the oven so that it is already warm. Stir
  until it is completely dissolved.
Boil rapidly until the jam sets, probably only
  about three or four minutes.
To test if it is set, place a teaspoon of jam on
  a chilled saucer. If it forms a skin the jam
  is ready. Pour the hot jam into warmed,
  clean jars and seal.

Blackcurrant jam

Ingredients:
1 lb / 450g blackcurrants
1 lb / 450g sugar
3/4 pint / 425ml water

Method:
Put the blackcurrants and water into a large
  pot. Simmer slowly for about 15 minutes
  until the fruit is tender.
Stir in the sugar and boil rapidly
  until the jam is ready to set.
Pour into warmed clean jars
  and seal.

Bilberry jam

Ingredients:
1 lb / 450g bilberries (also known as
    blueberries)
1 lb / 450g sugar

Method:
Put the bilberries into a large pot and simmer
    for about 5 minutes. Add the sugar and
    stir until it has dissolved.
Boil until the jam is nearly ready to set,
    watching it carefully as this jam sets quite
    quickly.
Pour into warmed clean jars and seal.

Bilberry muffins

Ingredients:
8 oz / 225g self-raising flour (a mixture of
    half white and half wholemeal)
2 oz / 50g caster sugar
1^1/$_2$ tsp baking powder
1 egg, lightly beaten
1 cup bilberries
3 oz / 75g melted margarine or butter
9 fl oz / 25ml milk

Method:
Preheat the oven to gas mark 6 (400°F /
    200°C).
Line 12 bun tins with paper cases.
Sift flour and baking powder into a large
    bowl. Stir in the sugar and the bilberries.
Melt the margarine or butter in a small pan.
In another bowl, mix the beaten egg, melted
    butter or margarine and milk.
Add the liquid to the dry ingredients and stir
    gently with a fork, being careful not to
    bruise the berries.
Spoon the mixture into each paper case, so
    that each is about 2/3 full.
Bake at gas mark 6 (400°F / 200°C) for 20-25
    minutes.
Cool on a wire rack.

Bilberry muffins are especially delicious if you

eat them while they are warm, with butter.

(You could also make Apple Muffins, by
using a cup of chopped eating apple instead
of the bilberries, and adding half a teaspoon
of ground cinnamon.)

The Auld Lammas Fair

At the auld Lammas fair,
    were you ever there?
Were you ever at the fair
    of Ballycastle, oh?
Did you treat your Mary Anne
    to dulse and yalloman
At the auld Lammas fair
    of Ballycastle, oh?

Yalloman or Yellow Man is a type of puffed
candy popular in the north of Ireland. Dulse
or dillisk is a red-brown sea vegetable that
can be eaten raw or cooked in soup.

Yellow man

Ingredients:
1 lb / 450g syrup
4 oz / 110g butter
1 lb / 450g brown sugar
1 tsp baking soda
2 tsp vinegar

Method:
Dissolve the sugar, butter, syrup and vinegar.
    Then boil without stirring until a drop
    hardens when dropped in cold water.
Remove from the heat and quickly stir in the
    soda. This will make it foam up. Pour into
    a greased tin and leave to cool.
Break into chunks. Store in an airtight tin.

At Lughnasadh, the first of the new crop of potatoes were dug and a pot of champ was cooked for the feast.

There was an old woman who lived in a lamp
She had no room to beetle* her champ.
She upped with her beetle and broke the lamp
And then she had room to beetle her champ.

* A 'beetle' is a wooden pounder for
    mashing potatoes.

Champ

Ingredients:
New potatoes
Scallions (Spring onions)
Butter and cream

Method:
Boil the potatoes and mash them with
    butter, cream and spring onions.
Serve hot, with a knob of butter in the centre.
    It is traditional to eat champ from the
    outside in, dipping each forkful into the
    butter first.

Things to do

Climb a mountain

Pack a picnic basket and climb the highest
hill in your area. Once you're at the top, play:

Toss the blanket – Six people hold a
blanket, three on each of two sides. One by
one each child lies in the blanket and is
tossed in the air, while the others call 'One,
two, three, up she goes.'

Originally a young couple who were courting
would have been tossed in the blanket
together.

Hold a pea fair

Look out your old toys and outgrown clothes.
Bake some buns. Lay them all out on a table
and hold a fair. Make some games, such as
The Pocket Lady, and **What's that smell?**
(see below).

Give each child a handful of peas. Charge
one pea per turn. There are plenty of peas
and everybody gets a turn. Here are some
pea fair ideas:

The Pocket Lady wears an apron with
twenty small pockets. Each pocket contains a
little treat, perhaps a sweet or a small trinket
or crystal. Small children love to pay a pea
and take a lucky dip into her pockets.

What's that smell? You will need five small
glass jars with lids and some strongly scented

materials. These could include curry powder, lemon peel, cloves, pepper, lavender, roses or ginger.

Put a different smell into each jar and close the lid. Wrap coloured paper around each jar so the contents can't be seen. Blindfold the child who has to guess what each jar contains. Remove the lid from each jar in turn and hold the jar under the guesser's nose.

Saving seeds

At this time of year the grains ripen. The seeds are ready to dry and store for the winter's food supply. In the old days it was important to save some of the grain so that there was seed to plant for next year's crop.

Although you may not be growing fields of oats or wheat, there are many flowers still in bloom. Some are now past their best and going to seed. For example, nasturtiums, marigolds (calendula) and sweet peas are easy seeds to save, as are beans and peas.

After the flowers have decayed and fallen, you will see the seed begin to form. They will swell and then begin to turn hard, brown and dry.

You can gather them up, leave in a warm, airy place to dry and then put them in an envelope. Write the name of the plant on the envelope, or draw a picture of it in bloom. Store in a dark, dry and cool place until it's time for planting again in the springtime.

Your own saved seeds in a pretty packet make a lovely gift for a gardener's birthday.

Horse races

In Ireland Lughnasadh was traditionally a time for horse fairs and races. In some places horses were raced through a river to give a blessing and protection.

There are still horse races on the seashore in some parts of Ireland today. You can carry on this tradition by having a day out at the beach and holding 'piggy-back' races on the beach.

Visit a spring well

A holy well is a natural ancient spring that was revered for the curative powers of its waters long before it became associated with an individual saint.

Over 3,000 holy wells are known in Ireland! Most became associated with a particular saint, for example, Tober Phadraig or Patrick's Well.

On the saint's feast day, a 'pattern' or patron is held at the well: people walk the rounds, a sunwise circuit around the spring, a prescribed number of times, usually three or nine times and then drink from the well. A handful of pebbles helps each person keep count of the rounds.

It is customary to leave behind an offering – a strip of cloth tied to a nearby bush, a coin or a rosary. Music, dancing, feasting and sports follow this ritual.

Most areas have their own holy well which is usually said to have a cure for headaches, eye complaints or warts.

You could find out where your nearest natural spring or holy well is. Walk to the spring and walk around it quietly, take a drink and leave a token offering, perhaps some flowers or a red ribbon tied to a bush. Then feast and celebrate with gingerbread, lemonade and fresh fruits.

Verbascum ear drops

Verbascum flowers between July and September. It is a tall plant, looking a little like foxglove, but with yellow flowers.

Pick the yellow flowers on a dry day.
Place in a jar and cover them in olive oil.
Keep the jar in a dark place for 2 to 4 weeks.
Strain and bottle. Use as eardrops so long as
the eardrum has not been broken.

Harvest

In rural Ireland the harvest was an occasion that brought whole communities together to carry out essential work while the weather was right. There was always some urgency about the work, and a great community feeling. This was one of the few times in the agricultural year when everybody had to work together.

The last sheaf left in the fields was known as the Cailleach, or the hag. In some areas it was considered an honour to cut this sheaf, while in other areas it was thought an ill omen. Sometimes there was a contest where reapers tossed their reaping hooks at the last sheaf.

Once cut, the sheaf was plaited or bound in an ornamental fashion and carried to the farmer with great ceremony. The farmer was

expected to provide a reward in the form of a great feast or harvest home.

The harvest home was usually held in a barn and the Cailleach was given pride of place. The barn was the only building large enough to hold all those who had helped with the harvest. The feast was followed by music and dancing, led by the girl who tied the last sheaf and the eldest son of the farmer.

Amongst Ulster Scots, the last sheaf was decorated and taken to the church for the Harvest Thanksgiving service.

Harvest Time

The boughs do shake and bells do ring,
So merrily comes our harvest in,
Our harvest in, our harvest in
So merrily comes our harvest in.

We have ploughed and we have sowed,
We have reaped and we have mowed,
We have got our harvest in.
Hip, hip harvest home!

Mother Goose

Festive food

Harvest loaf

Ingredients:
1 lb / 450g coarse wholemeal flour
1/2 - 3/4 pint / 275-425ml buttermilk
1/2 tsp salt
1/2 tsp bread soda

Method:
Mix the dry ingredients together.
Add enough buttermilk to make a wet dough. Knead lightly and quickly shape into a round.
Place in a greased 7-inch / 18cm round baking tin.
Cut a cross on the top with a sharp knife, dividing it into quarters.
Bake in a hot oven, gas mark 6 (400°F / 200°C), for 45 minutes, until it sounds hollow when tapped on the bottom.

Among the special items of food for the Harvest Home was a rice pudding made with milk in a pot oven. Yolks of eggs were whipped and poured over the top and this gave a tasty golden top to the pudding.

A pot oven, also known as a bastable, is a Dutch oven, a large heavy pot with a lid. The pudding was baked by piling red turf embers on top of the lid and underneath the pot

Rice pudding

Ingredients:
Cooked rice
Milk
Beaten egg
Sugar to taste
Grated nutmeg

Method:
Put the rice in a pot with the sugar and nutmeg. Add enough milk to cover it.
Simmer slowly in a pot until the milk is absorbed.
Turn into a casserole dish, pour the beaten egg over the rice and bake in the oven until it is golden.

Things to make

The harvest knot

At harvest time a simple form of the corn dolly was made, called a harvest knot. The harvesters wore them during their work and at the celebrations that followed.

Different knots were made for girls and boys. The girls' knots have the ears of corn and were worn in their hair, while the boys' have the ears removed and were worn on their coats. These knots would be exchanged as love tokens or 'favours'. This is the origin of the saying, 'Do me a favour'.

To make a harvest knot

You will need:
Four long hollow corn stalks with the ears
    attached.
20cm / 8 inches fine ribbon
Scissors
Heavy cotton thread in a colour to match the
    straw

Method:
Before you begin, you need to soak the corn
stalks in tepid water for at least 20 minutes.

Lay the four ears together and bind the
    stalks just below their ears.
Fold out the four stalks so that they point to
    the four points of the compass (N, S, E, W)

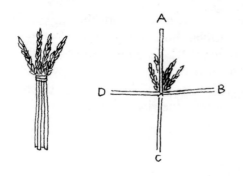

Fold stalk A so that it lies alongside stalk C.
Fold C so that it now lies where A was lying.

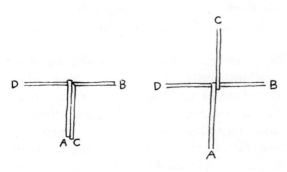

Fold B to lie beside D.
Fold D to where B was lying.

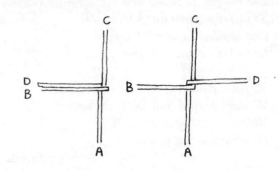

Repeat these four folds in the same order
    continuously, until you have only about
    5cm / 2 inches of stalk left.
Bind the end of the plait and then stretch it
    to even out any kinks.
Trim the ends of the corn stalks
Now you can coil your plait into one of a
    number of shapes – see diagram – and tie
    it in place with thread.
Use a length of coloured ribbon to tie a bow
    over the join.
Give your favour to someone you love!

Share your harvest!

It's a lovely idea, at this time of year to share
some of your surplus produce with others
who don't have a garden.

Basic salt dough

You will need:
3 cups white flour
3/4 cup salt
1 cup water

Method:
Mix the flour and salt thoroughly and then add the water. Knead the dough until it is flexible and without lumps.

Make into shapes and bake flat on an oiled baking tray for 1 hour at gas mark 3 (325°F / 165°C). When cooled give 3 coats of varnish.

A wheat sheaf decoration

Roll out seven 'sausages' of salt dough about 15cm / 6 inches long and the width of your little finger. These are the stalks for your sheaf.

Cut seven oval shapes about 5cm / 2 inches long for the ears of corn. Make cuts in these to represent the individual grains.

Join these to the stalks by pressing them together.

Place the seven stalks side by side and wrap a further length of dough around them to bind the sheaf together.

Bake in the oven and when cool, give three coats of varnish.

The Ripe and Bearded Barley

The leaves are turning yellow and fading into red,
While the ripe and bearded barley is hanging down its head.

All among the barley who would not be blithe,
While the ripe and bearded barley
Is smiling on the scythe?

The wheat is like a rich man, it's sleek and well-to-do.
The oats are like a pack of girls, they're thin and dancing too.
The rye is like a miser, both sulky, lean and small,
Whilst the ripe and bearded barley is the monarch of them all.

All among the barley who would not be blithe,
While the ripe and bearded barley
Is smiling on the scythe?

The spring is like a young maid that does not know her mind,
The summer is a tyrant of most ungracious kind.
The autumn is an old friend that pleases all he can
And brings the bearded barley to glad the heart of man.

All among the barley who would not be blithe,
While the ripe and bearded barley
Is smiling on the scythe?

Anon

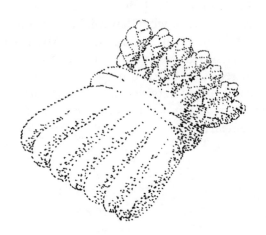

Michaelmas, 29 September

The feast of Michaelmas was not greatly celebrated in Ireland. Michaelmas was introduced to Ireland by the Anglo-Normans. Hiring fairs and mayoral elections were held at this time of year in areas influenced by the English. It was also a quarter day for gathering rents.

Michaelmas marked the end of the harvest, the end of the fishing season and the beginning of the hunting season. It was traditional to kill a goose at Michaelmas, also known as *'Fomhar na nGéan'*, or 'goose harvest'. Geese were plucked, and pillows and mattresses stuffed with new feathers. Sometimes a goose would be given as part of the rent, and it was also a time to give surplus geese or other produce, to the poor and needy.

There is a legend that Lewey, son of King Leary, was restored to life and health by St Patrick, acting under the intercession of St Michael. The queen, vowed to give one sheep from each of her flocks to the poor each Michaelmas day in thanks and so it became a custom for families to give to the poor at Michaelmas.

St Michael was known for two main things: Subduing the dragon and weighing the souls of the dead. Michaelmas is often a time of meteor showers, when 'cosmic' iron from the stars falls to earth, reminiscent of Michael's glinting sword. Michael teaches us to be courageous, to tackle our own inner dragons, to stand firmly between heaven and earth, to face the coming darkness of winter with a brave heart.

Michael the Victorious

Thou Michael the Victorious
I make my circuit under thy shield,
Thou Michael of the white steed,
And of the bright brilliant blades,
Conqueror of the dragon,
Be thou at my back,
Thou ranger of the heavens,
Thou warrior of the King of all,
O Michael the victorious
My pride and my guide,
O Michael the victorious
The glory of mine eye.

(from *Carmina Gadelica*, collected by
Alexander Carmichael)

Rent Day

*I*T WAS a bright and breezy Michaelmas day
and the sun seemed to dance on the surface
of the lough. Pat Moony sat on a rock by the
water's edge with his head low in his hands,
lamenting. Despite the pleasant weather of the
day, a hard summer had given him much grief.
His crops had failed and the butter was poor.
Annie and the children were thin as rakes and
hungry as howling wolves.

Today, O'Farrell, the landlord's agent
would be waiting for the rent: this
quarter's rent and what was owed from
the quarter before. Pat knew that if he
couldn't pay O'Farrell his every penny,
O'Farrell would put them out and turn
the farm over to his own nephew, Jack.
It was a grand farm at the best of times,
and O'Farrell's nephew had long had his
eye on the finest field.

'Ochone, ochone. What am I to do?'
groaned Pat.

A sudden rustling in the furze bushes
pulled Pat's gaze up from his work-worn
hands. There, before him, on a pure white
horse, sat the tallest and grandest of gentlemen.
He wore a fine black coat with long tails, a tall
black hat, a blue silk cravat at his neck, and
boots of black leather, polished so bright that
Pat could see his own miserable face reflected
in them.

'Whatever is the matter with you, my good
man, that you sit here lamenting on a fine
autumn day?' the gentleman asked.

Pat told the story of his failed harvest and
his hungry wife and children. He told the
gentleman that he must pay his rent by midday,
and it is now almost noon, and he not having a
penny to pay it with. And he told how O'Farrell
would surely seize the farm, and turn them out
to wander the roads as homeless beggars.

'A sad tale, my good fellow. But I can see by
your hands that you are not a man to shirk an
honest day's toil. Surely this man O'Farrell will
listen to your plight, and give you credit till
you're back on your feet again.'

'Sure, he might if he had an honest heart in
him, sir. But he has his eye on my finest field for
his own nephew Jack. There's no pleading with
the landlord's agent.'

The gentleman reached within his coat and
pulled out a richly embroidered purse. Pulling it
open he poured a stream of gold coins into Pat's
battered old upturned hat, saying, 'Here, good

fellow. Now go, pay your rent. Have no fear but your luck is changing.'

Now, Pat was astounded at the sight of the gleaming gold guineas in his ragged old hat. But, before he could rise to shake the fine gentleman's hand and thank him for his kindness, both man and horse had disappeared. All that could be seen was the blue heron circling overhead and a few ripples spreading on the surface of the lough. Pat called out over the water, 'A blessing on you, sir. Pat Moony gives his heartfelt thanks, wherever it is you've gone.'

So Pat set off at a proud pace to the landlord's agent to pay his rent.

O'Farrell sat behind his desk, a sneer curling his thin lips. 'Well now, Pat Moony, have you money for me today? I warn you, if there's but one penny short, you'll be packing your bags and out by nightfall!'

Pat walked tall and straight to the agent's desk, and looked O'Farrell proudly in the eye. 'There is your rent, O'Farrell,' he said as he tipped the gold guineas from his hat onto the agent's ledger book. 'You can count it out now and write me a receipt – for the back rent and all – it's all there, every penny.'

O'Farrell's eyes opened wide with surprise at the pile of golden guineas. He counted the coins, and when he saw it was correct, he took up his pen and wrote out Pat's receipt, two copies. Pat took his receipt, proud as a lion, secure in his home and farm, and suddenly confident in a brighter future. He walked out, leaving the door open behind him, and danced all the way home to tell Annie of the kindly gent and their good fortune.

Meanwhile, O'Farrell sat behind his desk with a puzzled look on his face. How had Pat Moony come by so much gold? He picked up a guinea coin and bit into it – it was real enough. If he hadn't seen those guineas with his own eyes, he'd have thought it was a trick.

A sudden gust of wind blew in the open doorway, and O'Farrell stepped up to close the door. Before he reached it, he heard behind him

a rustling like the sound of autumn leaves. He turned, and there on his ledger, he saw swirling in the breeze, not golden guineas, but a pile of dry, brown leaves. In two long steps he was back at his desk. He reached out his hand to pick up what should have been gold, and the breeze took the golden leaves higher and higher, always just out of his reach.

He chased the mocking leaves as they danced around the room. He stretched and gasped and leapt and turned, he twisted and stooped and spun and hopped, but he never quite caught up with the dancing leaves. One last puff, and the breeze swirled the golden leaves out the door and laughing down the lane.

O'Farrell puffed and panted to catch his breath. He sat down, dumbfounded and red in the face, and shook his head. There before him on the desk was the receipt for Pat Moony's rent, written by his own hand, signed and sealed and binding.

He knew there was little point in telling about the gold that turned to leaves. He would look the biggest fool in the parish if word of this got out.

From that day onwards, Pat Moony's cattle grew fat and his crops grew tall. Annie churned the finest yellow butter and her chickens laid the best brown eggs in the county. Their children grew bonny and fair and all that they began ripened to fullness.

And there's not one day goes by that he forgets to give thanks for his good fortune, and to give his blessing to the mysterious gentleman who changed his luck on rent day.

Festive food

Dragon bread

Ingredients:
1 lb / 450g wholemeal flour
1 tbsp oil
1 tsp dried yeast
1 tsp sugar or honey
Warm water
Raisins
Flaked almonds or pumpkin seeds

Method:
Dissolve yeast in warm water with the sugar or honey and leave to sit until it is frothy on top.
Put the flour in a large bowl and stir in the oil and the yeast mixture. Knead well and leave to rise until doubled in size.

Divide into several pieces, each piece will make one dragon. Knead each lump of dough and form each into a dragon's body. Make eyes by pushing raisins into the head.
Make cuts in the back for scales or spikes. Form a spiky spine by inserting a line of flaked almonds or pumpkin seeds.
Place on greased baking sheet and bake as for rolls, about 15 minutes at gas mark 7 (425°F/220°C).

Your dragon rolls will be lovely with a warming dish of Coddle, a straightforward and economical stew.

Coddle

Ingredients:
8 potatoes
4 onions
8 rashers of bacon
8 sausages
Vegetable stock
Salt and pepper to taste

Method:
Clean and thickly slice the vegetables. Place in a large pot with the rashers and sausages.
Pour in enough water to cover and bring to the boil. Add pepper and simmer for about an hour.
Sprinkle with parsley.

For a vegetarian coddle, leave out the rashers, add some thickly sliced carrot and use vegetarian sausages.

My wife would persuade me, as I am a sinner
To have a fat goose on St Michael for dinner
And then all year round, I pray you I mind it
I'll not want for money – oh grant I may find it!

An old rhyme from 1709 in Florence Irwan's
Irish Country Recipes from Ulster

Poor man's goose

Ingredients:
1 lb / 450g liver
1 tbsp flour
1 medium onion
1 tbsp water
1 lb / 450g potatoes
Salt, pepper, sage

Method:
Slice liver, and coat in flour.
Chop onion finely and layer in a greased dish with the liver. Season and moisten with water.
Top with peeled sliced potatoes.
Cook at gas 5 (375°F / 190°C) uncovered for ³/4 - hour.

Apple harvest

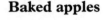

Baked apples

Per individual:
1 rosy eating apple
1 clove
Water
Sultanas

Method:
Remove the core and score around the skin at the apple's widest point. Place in an ovenproof dish.
Fill the hole at the core with sultanas, sugar and cloves. Put a little butter on top and pour over the water.
Bake for 30 minutes.

Storing apples for the winter

Don't try to preserve windfall apples, they'll probably be bruised. Hand-pick the best apples, handling the fruit as little as possible. If possible, pick them on a fine dry day. Wipe the apples to ensure that they are thoroughly dry, and reject any that are not perfect (eat them today or within the next few weeks!)

Store in a dark, dry place, in single rows, upon clean straw, with straw between each row. Make sure they are not touching each other.

Check them every now and then and remove any apples that seem to be going bad. It's true that one bad apple can spoil the whole store!

'La Fheile Mhichil a chroitear an t-ullord'
or 'At Michaelmas the orchard is shaken'.

It's time to begin using up all the apples!

Things to make and do

Dragon

You will need:
Green card
Red tissue paper

Method:
Copy the pattern for the dragon's body onto the green card and cut it out. Make a slit in the body for the wings to go through.

Cut a strip of red tissue paper 12 x 15cm (5 x 6 inches). Place in front of you with the narrower edge facing you.

Fold the tissue paper like a fan or concertina, using folds between 1cm and 1.5cms ($^1/_2$ to $^3/_4$ inch) wide.

Cut out diamond shapes at the folds. Fold the 'fan' in half and insert through the slit in the dragon's body until the midpoint is reached.

Spread the wings and join the two together at the top with the needle and thread, leaving a long thread for hanging the dragon.

Shooting star

You will need:
Piece of shining fabric
Matching thread
Thin ribbon or coloured strings
Needle and pins
Lentils, barley or rice to fill

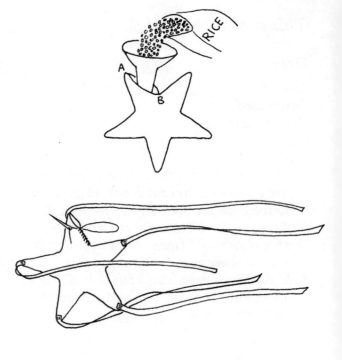

Method:
Photocopy the pattern. Fold the fabric in
    half and pin the pattern onto the cloth.
Cut out 2 stars following the cutting line.

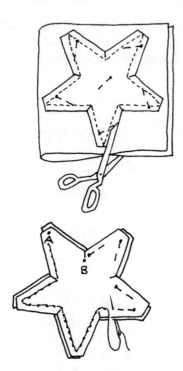

Catch a falling star!

This game is often known as Piggy in the
    Middle. It is played with three or more
    children. One (the Piggy) stands in the
    middle.

The others throw the beanbag to each other
    over the Piggy's head. If Piggy catches the
    beanbag before the child it was meant for,
    that child becomes the Piggy in the
    middle, and so the game goes on.

Pin the two stars together, matching points,
    with right sides facing towards each other.
    Sew the two stars together, leaving an
    opening at A-B.
Turn the right way out and fill with barley or
    rice. Carefully sew up the gap at A-B.
Cut the ribbon into five lengths and sew one
    onto each point.
When you throw the star, the ribbons will trail
    behind, like the tail of the shooting star!

Curiosities and Cures

Luck money

When selling something for cash at a fair or in a private bargain, it is traditional for the seller to give back a portion of the price as luck money. For example, a few years back I bought a second hand wood-burning stove for £50 and was given back £5 as luck money.

Fairy thorns

A fairy thorn is a hawthorn bush that has self-seeded and stands alone in a field away from any hedges. It is considered very bad luck to cut down a fairy thorn. The fairies would be upset and seek some revenge.

Within the last few years a planned stretch of dual carriageway in Co Clare was re-routed after local opposition to the removal of a fairy thorn.

A fairy fort is usually the remains of an ancient earthwork or ringfort, where the fairies are thought to have taken up residence. The same misfortune is thought to befall anyone who interferes with one.

Holy wells

The water in many holy wells is said to have healing properties, as cures for headaches, eye complaints or warts.

A charm against warts

Water found in a hollow stone or *bullaun* is a cure for warts. One should dip the finger in the water, rub it on the warts and speak this verse:

Water in the hollow stone, not to find you did I here come,
But since I met you here today I hope you'll take my warts away!

Within a week the warts should disappear.

Good luck charm

A stone with a hole in it is good luck and offers protection against the evil eye.

Smooring the fire

The fire was central to the home and was never to go out. Before retiring for the night, the woman of the house would rake and 'smoor' the ashes of the peat fire in the open hearth. She would bury a turf, still smouldering, under a pile of ash and draw a cross on the ashes. Next morning she could kindle a new fire from the spark of the previous day's fire. At Bealtaine and St John's Day, embers from the community bonfires were brought home to rekindle the family hearth.

Wake traditions

When a member of a household dies, a window or door is opened to allow the spirit to depart. The body is brought back to the house. A great deal of food and refreshments is brought in because for the next two nights the house is open to neighbours and friends to accompany the deceased through the dark hours of the night.

Music, song, dancing, games and storytelling surround the deceased, who is laid out in the best room of the house. Twelve candles are lit and kept burning throughout the two nights. In older days the wake lasted two or sometimes three nights.

Women, the elderly and children came to visit the body during the day.

At night it was the men who kept watch and played wake games. These games, tests of skill and strength, often designed to put the players into embarrassing situations, are a remnant of an old tradition of honouring the dead. Some games involve fertility symbols like bulls and cows and mock-marriages.

In one game a player was chosen as 'chairman'. He sat on a chair in the middle of the room while a second man knelt, blindfolded, at his feet with his head on the chairman's knees and one hand held, palm outwards behind his own back. The players try to slap his hand. The kneeling man had to guess who had slapped him. If he named the right person, that man would take his place. If he guessed wrong, the slapping continued and the game could become very rough.

Farewell

Now we have reached the end of the book, it is time to say farewell.

When we gather together with friends to celebrate the festivals, we don't want to spoil the special experience by rushing off without saying goodbye. The following traditional Irish verse offers a blessing from the four elements of earth, air, fire and water, wishing that each of us be safe until the next time we meet. A lovely, touching and appropriate way to say goodbye...

An Irish Blessing

May the road rise with you
May the wind be always at your back
May the sun shine warm upon your face
May the rain fall soft upon your fields
And until we meet again, may God hold you
In the hollow of God's hands.

Words: traditional
Music: Nickomo

This verse can be sung, with accompanying hand actions. Begin by standing together in a circle facing inward.

Music is on the next page.

Line 1: bring hands up as the road rises to meet you

Line 2: bring hands behind

Line 3: raise arms and draw them back down towards the face like the sun shining

Line 4: raise arms and bring down again with fingers as raindrops

Line 5: raise hands at sides, level with heart

Line 6: bring hands together in front of heart, left hand facing up, covered by right hand facing down, as if holding something very precious.

Appendix 1
A well-stocked crafts box

This could include:

squares of felt in several colours
small pieces of cotton fabric
balls of wool
sheep's fleece or wadding
sewing cotton
needles and pins
ribbon
scissors, secateurs and a craft knife
paper and card in a variety of colours
crayons, pencils, eraser, ruler
watercolour paints and paint brushes
PVA glue
paper glue
sellotape
twine or string
florists' wire
found objects such as pine cones, acorns,
pebbles, shells, crystals

Appendix 2
Appropriate ages for games and activities

Games and activities are arranged in chronological order, beginning with Samhain.

Game / activity   **Suggested appropriate age**

Autumn to Winter

Nutshells 7
Spell to reveal a true love's name 7
Snap-apple . . . . .5 for playing, but an older person needs to set it up.
Bobbing for apples . . . . All ages.
Fortune-telling .10
Dead Man Arise .4
Tir na Nog 10
Green Gravel 5
Black Magic . . . . .12 for the mind reader. Audience can be of all ages.
Turnip lantern . . . . .9 but 4 year-olds with adult help.
Parshell 9
Make your own broomstick . . . . .10 with adult supervision.
Decorative corner for a picture frame 8
Clip frame with Celtic design 8
Celtic knotwork border 10
Giveaway 10
Breathing in Peace 10
The Advent Garden . . . . .3 upwards can walk the garden. Adults set it up.
Candle apples . . . . Adults make these for children.
Advent wreath 8
Hanging wreath .10
Walnut shell Advent calendar . . . . Adults make these for children.
Christmas crackers 8
Celtic Christmas cards 10
Miniature pomander 5
Carved pomander 10
Chocolate apricots 10
Round gift box 9
Sleep sachet 9
Little Christmas stockings 5
Twelve days ring .8
Marzipan stuffed dates 4
Gardener's hand cream 10
Celebrate the solstice . . . . All ages.
Newgrange sunrise at home . . . . .12 with adults.
Turnip candle holder 9
Consequences 10
Art consequences 7

Game / activity	Suggested appropriate age
Biographies	8
Confessions	6
Predicaments and remedies	10
Winter bird cakes	9
Pine cone bird feeder	9
Gold gift box	8

Winter to Spring

St Brigit's crosses:	
Sunwheel or swastika type	7
Diamond cross	5
Interlace cross	9
Brideóg	7
Green Lady	4
Little shaped candles	5 with adult supervision.
Candle dipping	6
Rush light	6
Earth candle	8
Valentine card	4
Heart brooch	7
Heart baskets	6
Spring cleaning inside and out	7
Chickweed salve	10
Pin-on shamrock	7
Mother's Day gift box	7
Posy of flowers	4
Easter grass	3
Sprout seeds for salad	5
Nest for eggs	7
Watch the sun dance	3
Visit a holy well	All ages
Clúdóg	5
Rough and ready egg spoon	8
Egg hunt	3
Onion-dyed eggs	10
Egg rolling	2
Blowing eggs	7
Painting blown eggs	4
Woven paper basket	10
Mother hen and her chicks	6
An Easter border	7

Summer months

May bush	5
Simple flower garland	5

Game / activity	Suggested appropriate age
Flower garland 2	6
Floral crown	7
A May ball	12
In and out the dusky bluebells	3
Nuts in May	7
Ball games	7
Sack race	3
Three-legged race	3
Grinning or gurning	3
May dew for health and beauty	7
Gathering herbs	5
Drying herbs	5
Comfrey poultice	8
Turf modelling	5
May Day divination	7
Whitsun dove	4
Fair Rosa	4
Lavender favour	9
Sage smudging stick	7
Rose petal tincture	Adult.
Sunwheel mandala	10
Earth art mandalas	10
Spectacular sun fire wheel	Adults only.

Summer to Autumn

Pocket Lady's apron	10
Berry picking	4
Fairy basket	9
A horse of rushes or straw	6
Toss the blanket	4
Hold a pea fair	10
What's that smell?	6
Saving seeds	6
Horse races	4
Visit a spring well	6
Verbascum ear drops	Adult.
The harvest knot	7
Basic salt dough	7
A wheat sheaf decoration	7
Dragon	4
Shooting star	7
Catch a falling star!	6

Bibliography and further reading

This list is by no means an exhaustive bibliography, but just a few books that may be of interest.

Carmel O Boyle, *Cut the Loaf: The Irish Children's Songbook,* Mercier Press, 1986

Carey, D., Large, J.: *Festivals, Families and Food,* Hawthorn Press, 1982

Clancy, Padraigín (ed.): *Celtic Threads,* Veritas, 1999

Colum, Padraic: *The King of Ireland's Son,* Floris, 1997

Cornell, J. B.: *Sharing Nature with Children,* Exley Publications Ltd., 1989

Croker, Crompton: *Irish Folk Stories for Children,* Mercier 1983

Dames, Michael: *Mythic Ireland,* Thames and Hudson Ltd, 1992

Danaher, Kevin: *The Year in Ireland,* Mercier Press, 1972

Day, Brian: *Chronicle of Celtic Folk Customs,* Hamlyn, 2000

Evans, Estyn: *Irish Folk Ways,* Routledge & Keegan Paul Ltd, 1957

Institute for Feminism & Religion: *Brigit Resource Packs I and II*

Jacobs, J.: *Celtic Fairy Tales,* Bracken Books, 1990

MacMahon, Bryan: *Peig,* Talbot Press, 1983

MacNeill, Máire: *The Festival of Lughnasa,* Comhairle Bhealoideas Eireann,1982

McGowan, Joe: *Echoes of a Savage Land,* Mercier, 2001

Mahon, Brid: *Land of Milk and Honey,* Mercier, 1998

Marshall, Ruth (compiler): *Freeing the Spirit,* Cooleenbridge School, 1995

Meek, Bill: *Moon Penny,* Ossian Publications 1985

Merry, Eleanor: *The Flaming Door,* Floris, 1989

O Catháin, Séamus: *The Festival of Brigit,* DBA Publications Ltd., 1995

O Duinn, Sean: *Where Three Streams Meet,* Columba Press, 2000

O'Leary, Sean: *Christmas Wonder,* O'Brien Press, 1988

Streit, Jacob: *Sun and Cross,* Floris, 1993

Taylor, Alice: *To School Through the Fields,* Brandon Books, 1990

Toulsen, Shirley: *The Celtic Year,* Element Books, 1993

Walsh, Thomas F.: *Once in a Green Summer,* Mercier, 2001

Yeats, W. B. (ed.): *Irish Fairy And Folk Tales,* Picador, 1979

Young, Ella: *Celtic Wonder Tales,* Dover, 1995

About the author and illustrator

Ruth Marshall has been editor of 'Network Ireland' holistic magazine since 1995. She is a mother, poet, teacher and she loves to sing. She has celebrated Celtic festivals for at least 30 years. She has worked as a folklore collector in the Scottish Highlands, run a wholefood shop, been a puppeteer... and she has learned a great deal through her involvement with Raheen Wood Steiner School in Co Clare for the past 16 years.

Judith Evans is an artist living in Co Clare. She is a founder-parent of Raheen Wood School for Steiner Education. She helps run a small puppet theatre performing mainly in the Mid-West of Ireland.

Other books from Hawthorn Press

Festivals Together
Guide to multicultural celebration
Sue Fitzjohn, Minda Weston, Judy Large

This special book for families and teachers helps you celebrate festivals from cultures from all over the world. This resource guide for celebration introduces a selection of 26 Buddhist, Christian, Hindu, Jewish, Muslim and Sikh festivals. It offers a lively introduction to the wealth of different ways of life. There are stories, things to make, recipes, songs, customs and activities for each festival, comprehensively illustrated.

You will be able to share in the adventures of Anancy the spider trickster, how Ganesh got his elephant head and share in Eid, Holi, Wesak, Advent, Divali, Chinese New Year and more.

'The ideal book for anyone who wants to tackle multicultural festivals.'
Nursery World

224pp; 250 x 200mm
paperback
1 869 890 46 9

224pp; 250 x 200mm
paperback
0 950 706 23 X

Festivals, Family and Food
Guide to seasonal celebration
Diana Carey and Judy Large

This family favourite is a unique, well loved source of stories, recipes, things to make, activities, poems, songs and festivals. Each festival such as Christmas, Candlemas and Martinmas has its own, well illustrated chapter.

There are also sections on Birthdays, Rainy Days, Convalescence and a birthday Calendar. The perfect present for a family, it explores the numerous festivals that children love celebrating.

'It's an invaluable resource book' The Observer

'Every family should have one' Daily Mail

All Year Round

Christian calendar of celebrations
Ann Druitt, Christine Fynes-Clinton, Marije Rowling

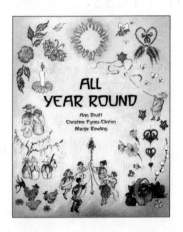

All Year Round is brimming with things to make; activities, stories, poems and songs to share with your family. It is full of well illustrated ideas for fun and celebration: from Candlemas to Christmas and Midsummer's day to the Winter solstice.

Observing the round of festivals is an enjoyable way to bring rhythm into children's lives and provide a series of meaningful landmarks to look forward to. Each festival has a special character of its own: participation can deepen our understanding and love of nature and bring a gift to the whole family.

320pp; 250 x 200mm; paperback; 1 869 890 47 7

The Children's Year

Seasonal crafts and clothes
Stephanie Cooper, Christine Fynes-Clinton, Marije Rowling

You needn't be an experienced craftsperson to create beautiful things! This step by step, well illustrated book with clear instructions shows you how to get started. Children and parents are encouraged to try all sorts of handwork, with different projects relating to the seasons of the year.

Here are soft toys, wooden toys, moving toys such as balancing birds or climbing gnomes, horses, woolly hats, mobiles and dolls. Designs and patterns for children's clothing are included, using natural fabrics. Over 100 treasures to make, in seasonal groupings.

192pp; 250 x 200mm; paperback; 1 869 890 00 0

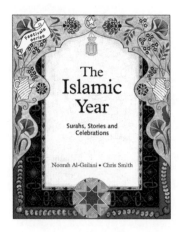

The Islamic Year
Surahs, Stories and Celebrations
Noorah Al-Gailani and Chris Smith

Celebrate the Islamic Year in your family or at school! You are invited to explore Muslim festivals with this inspiring treasury of stories, surahs, songs, games, recipes, craft and art activities. Folk tales illustrate the core values of Islamic culture with gentle humour and wisdom. *The Islamic Year* is beautifully illustrated with traditional patterns, maps and pictures drawn from many parts of the Muslim world, and Arabic calligraphy.

240pp; 250 x 200mm; paperback; 1 903458 14 5

Games Children Play
How games and sport help children develop
Kim Brooking-Payne
Illustrated by Marije Rowling

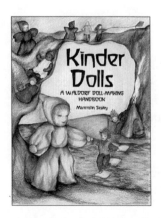

Games Children Play offers an accessible guide to games with children of age three upwards. These games are all tried and tested, and are the basis for the author's extensive teacher training work. The book explores children's personal development and how this is expressed in movement, play, songs and games. Each game is clearly and simply described, with diagrams or drawings, and accompanied by an explanation of why this game is helpful at a particular age. The equipment that may be needed is basic, cheap and easily available.

192pp; 297 x 210mm; paperback; 1 869 890 78 7

Kinder Dolls
A Waldorf doll-making handbook
Maricristin Sealey

Children treasure handmade dolls. Making a simple doll for a child is a gift for life, that encourages the magic of creative play. *Kinder Dolls* shows how to create hand-crafted dolls from natural materials. A range of simple, colourful designs will inspire both beginners and experienced doll makers alike. These dolls are old favourites, originating in Waldorf Steiner kindergartens where parents make dolls together for their children, and for the school.

160pp; 246 x 189mm; paperback; 1 903458 03 X

Storytelling with Children

Nancy Mellon

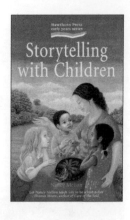

Telling stories awakens wonder and creates special occasions with children, whether it is bedtime, around the fire or on rainy days. Nancy Mellon shows how you can become a confident storyteller and enrich your family with the power of story.

'Nancy Mellon continues to be an inspiration for storytellers old and new. Her experience, advice and suggestions work wonders. They are potent seeds that give you the creative confidence to find your own style of storytelling.'

Ashley Ramsden, Director of the School of Storytelling,
Emerson College

192pp; 216 x 138mm
paperback
1 903458 08 0

Celebrating Christmas Together

Nativity and Three Kings Plays with stories and songs
Estelle Bryer and Janni Nicol

Create the wonder of Christmas with your children at school or at home – starting with a simple Advent Calendar and Crib Scene. This Treasury includes the Nativity Play, with staging directions and instructions for simple costumes and props, plus songs and music to accompany the play.

96pp; 210 x 148mm
paperback; 1 903458 20 X

'A practical and beautiful guide to making Christmas a magical time for children.'
Sally Jenkinson, author of *The Genius of Play*

Christmas Stories Together

Estelle Bryer and Janni Nicol

Here is a treasure trove of 36 tales for children aged 3-9. The stories range from Advent through Christmas ending with the Holy Family's flight into Egypt – in fact, tales for the whole year. These stories will soon become family favourites, with their imaginative yet down to earth language and lively illustrations.

128pp; 210 x 148mm
paperback; 1 903458 22 6

'This book is alight with the genius of storytelling. It tenderly shows how to weave a pattern of stories over Advent and the twelve days of Christmas.'
Nancy Mellon, author of *Storytelling with Children*

Pull the Other One!

String Games and Stories Book 1
Michael Taylor

This well-travelled and entertaining series of tales is accompanied by clear instructions and explanatory diagrams – guaranteed not to tie you in knots and will teach you tricks with which to dazzle your friends!

128pp; 216 x 148mm; drawings; paperback; 1 869 890 49 3

'A practical and entertaining guide, which pulls together a wealth of ideas from different cultures and revives a forgotten art. I think parents as well as children will enjoy this book.'

Sheila Munro, parenting author

Now You See It...

String Games and Stories Book 2
Michael Taylor

String Games are fun, inviting children to exercise skill, imagination and teamwork. They give hands and fingers something clever and artistic to do! Following the success of *Pull the Other One!*, here are more of Michael Taylor's favourite string games, ideal for family travel, for creative play and for party tricks.

136pp; 216 x 148mm; paperback; 1 903458 21 8

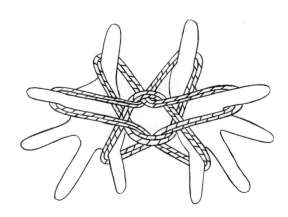

'Six-pointed star' from Book 1

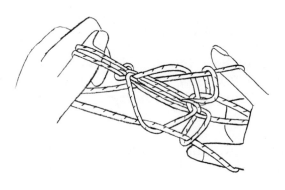

'The Frog' from Book 2

Free Range Education

How home education works

Terri Dowty (ed)

Welcome to this essential handbook for families considering or starting out in home education. *Free Range Education* is full of family stories, resources, burning questions, humour, tips, practical steps and useful advice so you can choose what best suits your family situation. You are already your child's main teacher and these families show how home education can work for you. Both parents and children offer useful guidance, based on their experience.

Here are:
- practical answers to questions such as 'how do they socialise?', 'money?', 'how do they take exams?', 'what about time for yourself?';
- inspiring blow by blow accounts with stories from 'home education' graduates about their jobs, training and lives; resources, contacts, networks and websites where you can get support;
- a friendly overview of the legal position to help you deal constructively with education authorities and find the advice you need;
- … and cartoons about Educating Archie for light relief!

256pp; 210 x 148mm; paperback; 1 903458 07 2

'Free Range Education *will encourage anyone contemplating the big step of going it alone…*'
Kids Out, August 2000

For further information or a book catalogue, please contact:

Hawthorn Press, 1 Lansdown Lane, Stroud, Gloucestershire GL5 1BJ
Tel: (01453) 757040 Fax: (01453) 751138 E-mail: info@hawthornpress.com
Website: www.hawthornpress.com

If you have difficulties ordering Hawthorn Press books from a bookshop,
you can order direct from:

Booksource, 32 Finlas Street, Glasgow G22 5DU
Tel: (08702) 402182 Fax: (0141) 557 0189 E-mail: orders@booksource.net

or you can order online at **www.hawthornpress.com**

Dear Reader

If you wish to follow up your reading of this book, please tick the boxes below as appropriate, fill in your name and address and return to Hawthorn Press:

☐ Please send me a catalogue of other Hawthorn Press books.

☐ Please send me details of Festivals events and courses.

Questions I have about *Festivals* are:

Name _____

Address _____

_____

Postcode _____ Tel. no. _____

Please return to:

Hawthorn Press, 1 Lansdown Lane, Stroud, Gloucestershire. GL5 1BJ, UK
or Fax (01453) 751138

IRF